THE PROFESSIONAL CARTOONIST'S BUSINESS MANUAL & MARKETING GUIDE

BY

DOUGLAS READY

THE PROFESSIONAL CARTOONIST'S BUSINESS MANUAL & MARKETING GUIDE

ISBN-13: 978-1548279103

ISBN-10: 1548279102

Published by **DMR Creative Enterprises.**

Printed and Distributed by **CreateSpace, a division of Amazon.**

www.douglasready.com

TO MONA

THE PROFESSIONAL CARTOONIST'S BUSINESS MANUAL & MARKETING GUIDE

THE CAREER CARTOONIST
ASSEMBLING A PROFESSIONAL PORTFOLIO
AGENTS, ATTORNEYS & OTHER PROFESSIONAL HAZARDS
STRUCTURING A SUCCESSFUL CAREER

PROFESSIONAL SUBMISSIONS GUIDELINES
     THE GAG PANEL
     THE COMIC STRIP
     THE COMIC BOOK & THE GRAPHIC NOVEL
     HUMOROUS ILLUSTRATION
     ADVERTISING, BOOKS & MAGAZINES
     GREETING CARDS & POSTERS
     PRODUCT DESIGN

THE CARTOONIST AS PUBLISHER
    WEBCOMICS
    THE CARTOONIST AND THE COMPUTER

COPYRIGHT, TRADEMARK & WORK FOR HIRE

LICENSING

BUSINESS LICENSES, TAXES & OTHER VARIOUS &
    SUNDRY ISSUES GUARANTEED TO CAUSE
    SLEEPLESS NIGHTS

TOOLS OF THE TRADE
    SAMPLE BILL OF SALE FOR ORIGINAL ARTWORK
    SAMPLE WORK FOR HIRE CONTRACT
    SAMPLE LICENSING CONTRACT
    SAMPLE SYNDICATION CONTRACT

A FINAL WORD

RECOMMENDED READING

ONLINE RESOURCES

THE CAREER CARTOONIST

Where do cartoonists come from? Everywhere!

Many of us at one time or another have been shoe salesmen, grocery store clerks, mail carriers, census takers, accountants, factory workers, ministers, bill collectors, bartenders, business executive, hardened criminals, politicians, lawyers, doctors, military personnel, exotic dancers and even unemployed.

Generally, we began drawing as children and never found anything quite as satisfying as the sound of someone laughing at one of our drawings. The more aggressive of us convinced aunts, uncles and grandparents to purchase some of those early cartooning efforts.

Some of us made the decision to pursue cartooning as a career. We marched forward, secure in the knowledge that our unique abilities would bring both fame and fortune in very short order. That mistaken notion is why so many of us at one time or another have been shoe salesmen, grocery store clerks, mail carriers...

There are only two ways to earn money as a cartoonist.

The first is to independently create a cartoon and find someone with the desire and the means to purchase that image. The second is to find someone with the desire and means to enlist your skills to generate an image that reflects their own imagination. In the first scenario, the cartoonist has sold a product. In the second, the cartoonist has sold a service resulting in the creation of a product.

One who creates comic or cartoon work designed from his own internal mechanisms is generally referred to as a Cartoonist. One who creates work designed to illuminate an idea generated by someone other than the cartoonist is generally referred to as an Illustrator, albeit a Humorous Illustrator. These descriptors are used to suggest a functional direction of purpose and nothing more. Both functions require a requisite amount of artistic talent and skill and inherent creativity. Both the Cartoonist and the Illustrator may well wind up producing the same kind of work, applying the same kind of skills and utilizing the same kind of working materials. Regardless of the arena in which one chooses to apply those skills, it is reasonable to consider both Cartoonists, and to consider both Artists.

As artists we are often presented with the notion that seriously attempting to generate a monetary return from what we produce is somehow beneath us--that exchanging our creative endeavors for financial gain somehow minimizes our accomplishments. Only in the creative sphere--and for some unfathomable reason especially the arena reserved for those of us who drag drawing implements across blank surfaces--is this concept given any serious consideration. Suggest to an automobile manufacturer or a pharmaceutical concern or even a movie production studio that their efforts are best geared toward the production of altruistic aesthetics--that they should profit from their labors only in a purely artistic sense--and they'll laugh your butt right off their respective premises.

And rightly so.

Nobody becomes a cartoonist just to make money. If financial return is the primary goal, there are a variety of methods guaranteed to help one achieve that end with a great deal less headache and less heartache, not to mention less aggravation. It is reasonable, however, to not only expect but also require that one's professional efforts consistently produce enough return to allow the regular acquisition of groceries and the disbursement of monies designated for rent, clothing, utilities and the occasional romantic foray.

CREATING AND SELLING CARTOON ART IS A JOB

A professional cartoonist is in effect an independent business operation, a manufacturing endeavor concerned with the concept and creation of an artistic product and the marketing and sales of that product. If the cartoonist lacks the ability to complete a reasonably unique project on a continuing basis, chances are his efforts will blend into the multitude of other proffered creative efforts and become lost in the shuffle, never allowing the gathering of a clientele anxiously awaiting the cartoonist's next work.

Likewise, if the cartoonist refuses to embrace the principles of basic marketing and learn elementary sales technique, chances are his efforts will never find the exposure necessary to build a dependable customer base.

A professional cartoonist understands the working aspects of his job, both functionally and philosophically. He strives to master those tools and techniques which will result in the creation of projects more likely to endear him to those who might purchase his work. He recognizes that a job is a continual process, lasting the full day and beginning again the next day, and knows that his job performance requires a critique not only in the area of artistic competence, but also in the areas of persistence, volume and follow through.

INVENTORY YOUR SKILLS

The cartoonist must be realistic about the achievement of his objective. He must make certain he has acquired the necessary skills he needs to be successful, and if not the cartoonist must be prepared to acquire those skills, both the artistic and the non-artistic.

There are certainly instances when an unqualified, less than competent creative hack has somehow managed to stumble into something that offers an incredible financial return on what little he has to offer. More often, success occurs when a practiced professional has taken the time to properly learn the application of the skills he's acquired and is recognized for his accomplishment.

ITEMIZE YOUR ATTITUDE

Ego is the biggest hurdle the working cartoonist must overcome if he is to have any chance of lasting success.

A certain pride in one's abilities and the willingness to acknowledge that the work produced is truly viable and valuable is essential to the cartoonist's survival, but the blind refusal to identify areas of less than stellar conception and execution and the unwillingness to engage in an improvement strategy to correct the problem will mark the cartoonist as something other than professional and guarantee a lifetime of pursuing what one can only hope will remain a satisfying hobby.

The cartoonist must learn to separate himself emotionally from the work he produces, if only for a period of time long enough to recognize that which must be improved. And, the cartoonist must learn to recognize when the required amount of improvement is so immense that he might actually be better off pursuing other venues.

For the cartoonist, there is no vision until that vision is shared. An unshared vision is merely a concept, lines on paper that will never enlighten, entice or entertain.

Continuous creation is paramount, if for no other reason the continuous application of skill is the only method of developing a truly unique and original personal style-- essential if the cartoonist is to not only survive, but thrive.

THE IMPORTANCE OF A BUSINESS PLAN

The single factor separating the professional cartoonist from the hobbyist is the intent to sell--intent, not desire. The professional structures his work schedule and his output to produce a required minimum amount of imagery to allow appropriate presentation to potential buyers.

The cartoonist must consider the possibilities inherent in his particular abilities and decide in what directions he will focus his creative efforts. Whether the cartoonist decides to produce self-conceived projects or whether he decides to pursue some faction of the commercial market, he will need to focus promotional efforts on his areas of choice.

Illustration assignments will most certainly not find their way to his studio unless they are directed there by an Art Director who's been informed of the cartoonist's abilities and availability. Interested publishers won't be revealed unless they've had the opportunity to learn of the cartoonist's abilities. The cartoonist must first identify those areas in which his skills suggest some viability, then target those areas he has an interest in pursuing. A preliminary business plan is nothing more than a written directive planning the creation and submission of work to various potential markets. The plan will necessarily include a time frame for completion of the different factions so the cartoonist may gauge his performance.

FUNCTION, PRODUCTION, PROMOTION AND PERCEPTION

There are many factors the cartoonist cannot control in his pursuit of financial solvency, especially in the beginning days of his career. The cartoonist must learn to focus on those areas that can be controlled, and control them to the best of his ability.

Function is directly controllable. The cartoonist is the one who determines that he will indeed spend a specified amount of time at the drawing board or easel, or devote a particular block of time to improving a specific skill.

Production is directly controllable. The cartoonist is the one who sets production deadlines, even if in the early stages of his career the deadlines are capricious.

Promotion is directly controllable. The successful cartoonist is the one who makes the effort to put his work in front of new prospects, and while there can be no guarantee of a sale there must certainly be a guarantee of a minimum number of presentations if the cartoonist is to find success.

Perception is directly controllable. The cartoonist is the one who must constantly reevaluate his skills--and his mindset--to make sure he is truly up to the task of continuously producing a viable product that can be successfully promoted and sold.

Simply put, making a living as a cartoonist comes down to these simple steps:

1. Learn your craft and practice it continuously.
2. Produce as much work as you possibly can and make sure the work that leaves your studio is the best work

you can produce. And make sure a LOT of work leaves your studio.

3. Never miss an opportunity for self-promotion. Understand that opportunity is MADE, not found.

4. Repeat Steps One, Two and Three every day, day in and day out for the rest of your professional working life.

Understand that the mediums you choose to work with today might not be the mediums that best showcase your abilities, and be open to making adjustments that will eventually serve you better.

Understand that every action will not bring a desired result. Know that rejection from any quarter is a temporary annoyance, nothing more and nothing less.

Review your work, your goals and your plan of action for achievement regularly. Retain what seems to garner a return, reject what doesn't. There are literally hundreds of different pathways to finding success as a cartoonist, and each of them is a valid route so long as you wind up at your chosen destination. If one approach isn't working for you, discard it and try another. And another. And another.

As my grandfather used to say: *You can't always get what you want, but you can generally get what you chase.*

ASSEMBLING A PROFESSIONAL PORTFOLIO

Your first publication will probably generate in your homctown. The local daily newspaper will buy a cartoon or offer to carry your comic strip, a local hamburger joint will need a new menu design, a local magazine or weekly newspaper will hire you to produce an editorial illustration or a local printer will begin referring requests for art and cartoon work toward you in exchange for an agreement that any work referred will be printed at his facility. You'll need a mechanism for presenting your abilities to these potential clients, a collection of samples to demonstrate your acquired skills.

An effective portfolio is a professional case designed to hold and showcase and protect the cartoonist's work. Artwork is secured inside acetate sleeves which will allow complete visibility, yet protect the work from damage caused by spilt coffee, smeared thumbprints and the odd ink smear. A good size for most cartoonists is a zippered case designed to hold up to a fourteen inch by seventeen inch piece of art, that is, large enough to hold an original comic book page. Anything larger than that is probably best showcased as a reduced reproduction.

A portfolio is not two pieces of cardboard wrapped with strings and rubber bands desperately attempting to hold the scraps of artwork tucked between the covers. If the cartoonist doesn't care enough to present his work in a professional manner, no Art Director or Editor is going to give the work or the cartoonist any serious consideration.

The professional portfolio holds twelve to twenty pieces of the cartoonist's most impressive work, pieces that not only show his or her skills to best advantage, but also demonstrate the variety of materials and genres the cartoonist has mastered. Less than twelve pieces indicates a beginner, possibly even a hobbyist who hasn't yet decided to become serious enough about cartooning to produce enough work to appear professional.

More than twenty pieces suggests a lack of confidence in the work included and a hope that overwhelming the viewer with sheer volume will somehow overshadow the cartoonist's inadequacies.

If the cartoonist has a proficiency in more than one area, samples should be grouped accordingly. Editorial illustrations should be filed adjacent each other, not scattered intermittently amongst comic book pages, menu designs and greeting card illustrations. Arrange the contents to showcase your best work in one genre, then move on to your best work in another genre.

Never leave a portfolio stocked with original art in the hands of a potential client. You'll want to leave printed material , specifically the same printed material you'd mail to potential clients you can't meet with face to face.

BUSINESS CARD AND STATIONERY

The business card serves as a record of contact information for the cartoonist as well as a reminder of the cartoonist's working style and abilities.

An effective business card reproduces an appropriate example of the cartoonist's work, as well as his name, address, telephone number and web address, all printed on the same side of the card. The text should be large enough and simple enough to easily decipher without the use of a magnifying glass. The card is professionally printed on a reasonably thick cardstock, not home printed on pre-cut templates that print slightly askew and allow ink to run down the holder's fingers should the card become damp.

If the cartoonist's overall work is primarily rendered in color, the art on the card should be printed in color. If the work is primarily black and white, or if it's a toss-up, the cartoonist will need to decide which sample best illuminates his abilities and proceed accordingly.

Thanks to digital printing, the cartoonist can secure copies of the card in bulk for a minimal investment, which is a good thing because at least in the early stages of a cartooning career--the cards should ideally be given to each and every person the cartoonist comes into contact with. Many of us have learned the hard way that you just never know when the guy you chatted with waiting in line at the neighborhood coffee shop is married to a lady whose brother's girlfriend is the Art Director at an ad agency.

Stationery should graphically match the business card. You can set up a stationery dummy in any Word Processing program on your computer, save the blank and print as you use it, which is much less expensive than ordering in bulk.

MAILERS

Assuming you don't live in one of the larger metropolitan media areas such as New York, Atlanta or Los Angeles, most of your initial contact with potential clients will be in the form of mailed samples.

A good rule of thumb is to reproduce three pages of your work, four samples on each page. Each page should be clearly identified with your name and contact information, your web address and a notice of copyright for the material presented.

Enclose a cover letter indicating your working experience--no resumes--and a statement of desire to work with the potential client and the availability to do so. If your working experience is limited, be honest about it. Most anybody you want to work with has undoubtedly been around long enough to spot a phony.

Make sure to attach two business cards. Responsibilities often duplicate within the walls of business, particularly in publishing and advertising, and you want to make sure an Editor or Art Director can easily pass information on to a cohort if he thinks the information might be useful.

THE WEB PORTFOLIO

The website's sole function is to effectively showcase the cartoonist's work. Regardless of the design specifications and functional anomalies, the web site must load quickly, capture the viewer's attention within just a few seconds, be easy to maneuver through and readily demonstrate the desirability of the artwork displayed.

Aesthetics are important to creative people and sometimes there is a tendency to focus more on the creation of the web site than its function. Whirling bits of animation, complicated mazes of boxes designed to lead the viewer from one gallery to another or pop-up boxes designed to regale the viewer with whatever visual wizardry conceived by the web designer who took your money are virtually guaranteed to drive away potential clients and prevent his or her return.

Imagine yourself standing inside a retail store at a magazine rack. If inflated promotional objects popped out at you every time you attempted to remove a magazine from the rack for consideration or if the rack began to spin every time you reached for a magazine, you'd probably leave.

So will most web surfers.

The idea is to make it as easy as possible for the potential client or customer to peruse your work. Remember, he isn't there because he's looking to be impressed with your marvelous ability to create a website. Don't let the web site become so annoying that actually looking at your artwork is the last thing a visitor would consider.

It's been estimated that you've got around four seconds to capture a web surfer's attention, *if you're lucky*. Every loading delay you build into your site increases the possibility that he'll be gone before the entire site is visible.

Don't assume most visitors have high-speed internet access.

If you're selling product from your website--original art, posters, greeting cards-organize the site into two sections: a portfolio section and a catalog section. Visitors who are considering contracting you for commercial services aren't generally interested in wading through the thirty poster images you're pushing.

A variety of online companies seek to partner with creators to produce and sell product based on the creator's original art. Companies like Cafe Press and Lulu offer the opportunity to place your designs on products they produce and sell for a commission through their own web site. While a real opportunity for profit to the creator can be dubious, most of these companies offer a free web page to showcase your images on their products and will allow you to post a link to your own web site on that page.

Your website is one of the most effective--and inexpensive--marketing tools at your disposal. It gives you the opportunity to put your skills and the results of those skills in front of everyone in the world that has access to a computer twenty four hours a day, seven days a week--and all without printing or mailing costs.

BUILDING A CAREER

A professional cartoonist understands that artistic creation, if it is to be more than an exercise in a solitary and even self-congratulatory pursuit, must be approached on a daily basis as an endeavor designed to enhance the monetary standing of the participant.

In other words, it's a job.

The cartoonist must actively endeavor to acquire those skills not only imperative to producing the imagery so dearly important to him, but also the skills necessary to assure that the finished product is adequately displayed to a customer base. Many of us spend years learning the subtleties of applying inks and colors, but neglect--or even outright refuse--to learn the basic principles of marketing and sales, feeling that embracing these particular abilities is somehow beneath us, somehow taints our creative purity.

The simple truth is that the cartoonist who refuses to embrace the principles of basic marketing and learn elementary sales techniques seriously--perhaps terminally-undermines the possibility of finding the exposure necessary to build a dependable collector list or customer base.

The successful cartoonist realizes that building a career is a daily pursuit.

AGENTS, ATTORNEYS & OTHER PROFESSIONAL HAZARDS

Art Agents don't do anything for the cartoonist the cartoonist cannot do for himself, and probably more effectively. Let me say that again, emphatically: *Art Agents don't do anything for the cartoonist the cartoonist cannot do for himself, and probably more effectively.*

Most agents will tell you differently.

The baton for directing your career is probably best left in your own hands. I'm quite certain there's an agent out there who's worth every penny of the 20-25% you'll wind up paying him--plus expenses, in most cases--but in thirty-plus years in the art business, I've yet to meet him.

It isn't that art agents are inherently evil, it's just that they usually aren't necessary. There are instances when an art agent's negotiating skills could work to the cartoonist's advantage, but negotiation skills--like sales and marketing-- is an attribute reasonably easy to acquire. Dropping your career development strategy into anyone's hands other than your own can be a recipe for disaster. Any agent generating enough commission to earn a living from his efforts must by necessity represent a stable of cartoonists, thus defusing his efforts to enhance a single career. The cartoonist who refuses to accept responsibility for building his own career often discovers that he has become just another notch on an agent's list and is missing out on important opportunities simply because he himself isn't chasing them.

And forget about signing with an agent and continuing to chase appropriate work yourself. The industry standard is for the agent to require his full commission on *any* project the cartoonist tackles while signed, regardless of its source.

In the greatest majority of cases, art directors are directly approachable. The cartoonist willing to assume responsibility for marketing his own abilities and negotiating his own pay rates will usually have a more secure and successful career than the artist who shoves that responsibility in another direction, crosses his fingers and hopes for the best.

That said, there is one area where an agent can significantly increase the probability of success: book publishing. If your ambitions include writing and illustrating children's books--assuming you're looking to create your project from scratch, not just to secure an illustration assignment from a publisher--or humor books or even how-to art books, an agent is often a necessity for securing the best working contract.

Please note the difference between the Literary Agent and the Art Agent. If you're trying to sell a book, you don't want the presentation and the negotiations handled by someone whose primary experience is hawking your drawing ability to an ad agency.

Access to an attorney with experience in intellectual property, specifically art and design, is paramount. Attorneys specialize in different areas of law, and even in different areas of contract law. Think of it in medical terms: you wouldn't trust a Proctologist to surgically remove your tonsils, and you don't want to trust an attorney without experience dealing with those areas that will directly affect your career and your income. Take the steps now to identify several attorneys with appropriate experience before you need to speak with one of them--that way, you know who to call. In a crisis situation, you're more likely to settle for an attorney who just isn't qualified to properly deal with your concerns.

Eventually, once you begin to achieve some measure of success in selling your artistic endeavors, you'll find yourself confronted by any number of promoters, referrers, coordinators--in short, people who neither purchase art outright nor offer assignments-who will assure you they can enhance your visibility by introducing you to any number of potential clients. You'll also find that any number of art agents who wouldn't consider adding you to their roster prior to your self-won published accomplishment are now miraculously enchanted by your work and are certain they can manage your career a good deal more effectively than you've managed to do on your own.

If you're bound and determined to hand the reins of your career over to someone else, at least use some common sense. Any agent asking for more the fifteen percent (15%) of the work he or she specifically generates for you should probably be sidestepped.

Licensing Agents generally want fifty percent (*50%!!!!!*) of whatever licensing deal they drum up. Brings to mind P.T. Barnum's most often quoted remark.

Get everything in writing--dollar amounts, percentages, payment schedules, copyright ownership, and-- just as important--specific terms for terminating the relationship.

And one more rule of thumb: **anybody who asks for money to promote you should be immediately dismissed.**

STRUCTURING A PROFESSIONAL CAREER

The biggest misconception about professional cartooning is that the job is to create cartoons. The job is to sell cartoons--creating them is just the preamble.

The second biggest misconception about cartooning is that the drawing is the most important aspect of the project. A quick look at the newspaper comics page, the cartoon-style ads in magazines or the contents of a great many alternative comic books will quickly reveal that there a great many successful cartoonists out there who didn't achieve their cartooning ambitions by trading on drawing ability--yet, there they are, some of them quite famous and generating a considerable wealth from the work produced. Why?

They've mastered the art of storytelling.

Cartooning is a primarily a communications art, not a strictly visual one. If your goal is to simply produce attractive or even intriguing imagery, I might suggest you spend time acquiring the skills to manipulate acrylics on canvas and pursue the gallery market. You'll greatly increase your chances of a successful career.

Cartooning is about communicating a message. Your finished project might contain the best artwork you've ever produced, but if it doesn't communicate anything no editor or publisher will touch it. The message might be a gag panel intended to make the viewer smile, an ad designed to entice a product's purchase or it may be an extended chronicle detailing the adventures of a comic book character, but without a message-without a story--it isn't a cartoon, it's merely lines on paper.

The professional cartoonist is the one who becomes proficient at storytelling. Generally speaking, most cartoonists spend at least a much time writing the material their comic will be based on as they do producing the finished drawing.

Acquire some basic writing skills. A class at a Community College can be a great benefit, but if this isn't practical a personally directed self-study course will go a long way toward improving the cartoonist's projects. Keep a good dictionary, thesaurus and English grammar book handy. Cartoonists often break the rules of writing, but it's helpful to at least know the rules so you can break them properly.

Write the story before drawing the pictures. Whatever message you're trying to convey, write the dialogue you intend to use before roughing out the art. Edit down the verbiage and reduce the number of words used. Remember, the artwork will work in conjunction with the dialogue to convey your message.

This doesn't mean that a good drawing style isn't an important aspect of a cartoonist's success. Yes, good storytelling will sometimes override less than exciting artwork, but the very best cartooning is a combination is good storytelling coupled with dynamic art.

As with any art form, cartooning is relatively subjective, that is, what might appeal visually to one person cannot be depended on to appeal to everyone. That said, an appealing drawing style is the second most important weapon in the cartoonist's arsenal. Simply, an effective drawing style entices the viewer to explore the cartoonist's effort.

To become a success, the cartoonist must develop a unique and consistent style, not just in the way the pictures look, but also in the way the stories are told. It might seem that working in a variety of styles would allow the cartoonist a wider audience, but the truth is that your own distinct, recognizable style is what will make your work better known.

Rock musicians generally play rock music for an audience, and it's rare to find a rock group that tosses in an operatic selection for a little variety. Likewise, working in a variety of styles dilutes the cartoonist's efforts. Art Directors and publishers--and the general reading audience, for that matter--will come to recognize and remember a drawing style long before they commit the cartoonist's name to memory.

The stronger his or her drawing and rendering skills, the wider the range of opportunities for the cartoonist, so developing a strong artistic ability is a priority. Art classes are one way of acquiring these necessary rendering skills, but many if not most cartoonists are self-taught artists. Fortunately, we live in an age when information on just about any subject matter is readily available. The local bookstore or library is overflowing with volumes on most any material and technique the cartoonist might wish to explore,, and there are a number of free Internet tutorials available on sites such as YouTube.

You'll learn much more much more effectively by studying art, not just cartooning. Composition, perspective, balance, color theory and the practical application of materials are often much more obvious in artistic works than in the cartoon counterparts, although most if not all of the same principles apply in the production of an effective cartoon. Experiment with different media and different styles. Experimenting is the only way to discover something natural and comfortable that will adapt to the work you produce.

There are a great many published volumes on the subject of producing cartoon drawings. Most are geared specifically toward reproducing the artwork contained in the book. Remember that the idea is to acquire a personal skill-set, not to simply mimic the work found between the covers of the text. Copying the artwork you find in these volumes can sometimes be a helpful exercise, but eventually the cartoonist if he or she is to move into the professional arena must begin to create his own unique style and characters.

If you want to become a novelist, you've got to spend a healthy chunk of your time reading novels because that's the only way you'll come to truly understand the form and begin to understand what might appeal to an audience. Likewise, if you want to become a cartoonist, you've got to spend a healthy chunk of your time reading cartoons.

If your goal is to produce gag panels, you've got to devour those current magazines and newspapers that purchase gag panels. Reading reprinted compilations, while often an enjoyable pursuit, is generally not a reliable way to gauge a current market because times and tastes change quickly and have undoubtedly changed between the time the cartoon was originally published and the time it was reprinted. If finding your work printed inside a comic book is your ultimate goal, you've got to spend a great deal of time actually reading the comic books currently available, studying the styles and the content. And if you want to create advertising cartoons, you got to constantly peruse those mediums that feature ad work.

Nobody will hire you unless they can see the sort of work you do. Developing a portfolio gives you the opportunity to show a potential client what you are capable of. It communicates how well you can communicate a message, what sort of style you have, the sorts of characters you use and, ultimately, whether you are suitable for the particular job a client has in mind.

You'll need to develop an effective web presence. An online gallery of your work can catch the attention of potential clients worldwide and thanks to email sending a scan of the finished cartoon work is often acceptable.

You'll also want to explore the possibilities inherent in self-publishing. Every cartoonist, regardless of his or her area of specialization, has one poster or half-a-dozen greeting card designs that could conceivably do quite well if sold exclusively from the cartoonist's website.

The successful cartoonist is the one who has taken a good, hard look at his abilities and realistically determined the specific markets that will best support his efforts to generate an income from his output. If your most effective and primary work is rendering cute cartoon sexpots, the cartoonist should understand that it is probably a waste of time to submit those samples to children's book publishers. Likewise, if the cartoonist has a flair for rendering cartoon animals, the men's magazines might not be the best market to pursue. Define your targets and aim appropriately.

Diversification is the key to developing a successful cartooning career. The cartoonist who takes the time to develop a strong drawing ability and strong storytelling skills is one who can effectively produce work for a wide variety of clients. It has been said there is a market for everything, and that may well be true, but that certainly doesn't mean there is a large market for everything, and it doesn't mean that any given market will have a need for a particular cartoonist's skill at any given point in time. The cartoonist who can effectively produce editorial or advertising illustration as well as effective comic pages has a definite advantage over the cartoonist who has developed an expertise in a single arena. The greater the number of genres your particular style can be adapted to, the greater the number of opportunities available to you.

IDENTIFYING POTENTIAL CLIENTS

There are a number of directory sources, such as the Better Business Bureau, that might also prove useful in identifying local clients. Local advertising agencies and weekly newspapers have served to launch any number of cartooning careers. The pay is seldom stellar, but it gives the beginner published experience and the start of a published portfolio.

And don't forget to contact your local comic book shop. You never know who is hanging around or visiting on a promotional tour, and your work hanging in this venue can be very beneficial. At the very least, it can provide opportunities to network with other cartoonists in your area.

IDENTIFYING WORLD-WIDE CLIENTS

The cartooning industry standard for the working cartoonist to source potential clients is the *Artists Market*. This nominally priced annual volume is now available in several different varieties, including the Children's Writer & Illustrator's Market. These volumes are not necessarily complete within themselves, but they do offer contact information for a substantial portion of the markets available to the fine artist, the illustrator and the cartoonist .

The Advertiser's Index is an invaluable source book for the cartoonist/illustrator interested in advertising or product design. This annual volume lists every company in the United States that spends a minimum of $50,000 a year on advertising. Contact information on each company usually includes the art director and the product development director, as well as information on which advertising agency handles that company's account. This book is expensive--better than $1000 a copy--but the business section of most public libraries will have a copy available. *The Standard Directory of Advertisers* is a good second source.

Any number of industry trade journals publishes an annual directory. *Toys, Hobbies & Crafts*, for example, publishes a toy industry directory that includes contact information on manufacturers, distributors--helpful for the entrepreneurial cartoonist who has decided to use his design skills to produce and market a functional product-importers, specialty design firms and licensing firms--helpful if you've developed a character you'd like to license across the board for use on existing product. Specialized business information can be pricey, so it is recommended the artist check the business section of his local library before purchasing these directories.

The publications necessary to build your career depend on the specific areas you intend to pursue. If you enjoy producing humorous illustrations and posters or prints are of interest--and a variety of cartoonists have done quite well in this market--*Art Business News* should be on your reading list. If comic books and graphic novels beckon to your creative abilities, *The Comics Journal, Diamond Distributor's Previews* and *The Comic Buyers Guide* should come in once a month.

A quick Internet search on any specific discipline of artistic endeavor using the Google search engine (www.google.com) will direct the artist to any number of specific, appropriate and viable referral sources, as well as potential clients to contact.

There are any number of creative directories--such as *American Showcase* or *Creative Illustration* in which the cartoonist may showcase his work. Hopefully, these directories wind up in the hands of an art director looking to hire. The cartoonist needs to carefully weigh the cost of inclusion in these directories before committing himself. These kinds of directories can prove helpful, but an effective, properly targeted direct marketing program can often produce the same kind of results at a more reasonable cost.

Cartooning is a business, and a business survives by making a profit. That profit is generated by creating and producing a product or service, then promoting and selling that product or service, over and over again. Every working day is structured to accomplish these ends. Financial solvency permits the continuation of artistic pursuit. A dedicated, straightforward approach to producing work and selling it permits financial solvency.

And, if the target is financial solvency, the cartoonist must target his efforts to produce the best possible results. The cartoonist must recognize his own creative ability, but he must also recognize that the presence of creative ability, even a powerful amount of it, will not generate a financial return unless that ability is properly and consistently applied to the creation of art, and the art produced is continuously presented to potential purchasers.

The cartoonist can spend a great deal of time and effort perfecting those skills necessary to produce wonderful work, but if no one knows what he can do he won't make any money at it. It really is that simple. Potential buyers have to know who you are, where you are, what you do and how to contact you.

A good rule of thumb is the 70/30 rule: 70% of the cartoonist 's working time is spend in the conception and creation stages of his career and 30% of the cartoonist's working time is spend promoting his skills and his product. Assuming the cartoonist 's skills are up to par, promotion is the key factor to securing a viable career.

It's important that promotion time is actually spent promoting. Lollygagging in front of an open *Artist's Market* sipping hot cocoa while talking on the phone to an intended romantic conquest isn't productive, and it surely isn't going to get the cartoonist where he wants to be. Promotion time should be spent actively researching potential markets and assembling the appropriate material to mail.

The cartoonist unwilling to aggressively promote himself, his talent and his product will never find continuing financial success as a professional cartoonist. In the cartoon business--just like any other business--you get no more than what you ask for. If you don't ask, you don't get anything.

A WORKING BUSINESS PLAN

Cartooning is a business.

The successful cartoonist is the one who devotes an appropriate enthusiasm and continuous activity to creating, producing and marketing his product. The successful cartoonist understands that the creative process is important, but no more important to his success than the daily application of business activity.

A working business plan is nothing more than an explicit statement of intent, a specified plan of action and detailed outline of the steps necessary to achieve this directive. It necessarily includes a time-frame for completion of the different factions so the cartoonist may gauge his performance.

If the cartoonist's goal is newspaper syndication for a new comic strip, the working business plan would expressly detail production goals (when the sample package will be completed) and promotion goals (when and to whom the completed sample package will be presented). There are certainly factors the cartoonist cannot control when dealing with a purchase decision that must be made by another party, but production and promotion are directly controllable. The plan should also include an alternate approach
for use of the material should the initial market offering, in this case newspaper syndication, prove unsuccessful.

No working business plan should focus exclusively on one project. The greater the volume of material the cartoonist has in circulation at any given time, the better the chances that some of his material will land in the hands of someone who not only appreciates it, but has a need to purchase it.

If the cartoonist's goal is to secure humorous illustration assignments, the business plan would include a set schedule for submitting samples to specific markets and lock in a time-frame to follow-up on those submissions.

SUBMISSION AND SUCCESS

The fact is that clients, at least in the early stages of your cartooning career, will not come to you. You've got to go to them.

It doesn't matter whether your particular offering is a finished product ready for publishing or the offering of rendering services to illuminate an Art Director's latest inspiration, the only way you'll begin to acquire and build a client list is to put yourself and your work in front of as many potential buyers as possible.

Probability plays an important part in any career, and cartooning is no different. If the cartoonist offers a gag panel to ten appropriate magazine markets, he has ten chances of selling it. If he offers the gag panel to thirty appropriate magazine markets, he has thirty chances of selling it. And, if he offers the gag panel to a hundred specialized magazines whose readers would have no interest in the cartoon's subject matter or to magazines that don't publish gag panels, the cartoonist has absolutely no chance of selling it.

PROFESSIONAL SUBMISSIONS GUIDELINES

The submission guidelines presented here are generally accepted formats and amenable to the majority of publishers, syndicates and advertising agencies. Of course, there are those potential clients who have specific submission requirements that may differ from these guidelines. A quick check of *The Artist's & Graphic Designer's Market* or the publisher's website will usually reveal any anomalies.

THE GAG PANEL

Modern gag panel format came to be thanks to the design requirements of *The New Yorker* magazine. The magazine formalized structure in order to maximize effective design of their magazine, then proceeded to hire some of the most talented cartoonists available to fill those pages with sparkling wit.

Gag panels are generally submitted in multiples of six. The cartoonist will do better in the early stages of his career by submitting six finished cartoons ready to print for the Cartoon Editor's review. Assuming the cartoonist's drawing abilities are not in question, the selling point of the cartoon is the joke. As the cartoonist builds a continuing relationship with a particular editor is may become acceptable to submit roughs--quick sketches detailing the joke--in which case the editor will request a finished drawing for those gags he wishes to purchase.

Never submit original cartoon drawings for consideration. The standard is to submit good quality photocopies or a printed copy of your own computer scan. Package a copy of each of the six cartoons unfolded into a nine inch by twelve inch envelope and include a self-addressed stamped envelope for the return of your drawings. Make certain to note your name and contact information on the back of each individual cartoon.

A cover letter isn't necessary.

When a package returns, immediately package whatever cartoons aren't purchased and send them off to the next potential buyer.

Some cartoon markets *Pay on Acceptance*, which means they cut the cartoonist a check when the decision is made to publish the cartoon. Others *Pay on Publication*, which mean they don't pay the cartoonist until the cartoon has actually been published. Conceivably, a market could hold your cartoon for months, even years, without paying you and if they later decided not to publish it, well, you're just out of luck. The *Artist's Market* will generally state a market's payment policies.

When a cartoon sells, send the editor a short Thank You note. Common courtesy goes a very, very long way. Anything you can do to help the editor remember you and your work is certainly to your benefit.

THE COMIC STRIP

The comic strip developed in America towards the end of the nineteenth century, originally created as a tool to draw customers to the Sunday edition of the local newspaper.

Thanks to mergers and takeovers, the number of daily

newspapers in the United States has dwindled to a fraction of the number of independent papers published in the 1950s and 1960s. The printed size of the comic strip continues to shrink, as does the number of strips published in the average daily newspaper. It is commonly accepted that the days of a new comic strip reaching the lofty ranks of the thousand paper stage have probably passed.

Syndication is often considered to be the upper echelon of cartoon success. The cartoonist chasing syndication has been compared to the actor chasing movie stardom--the rewards can be extraordinary, but only a talented few will reach that grand plain.

If a strip is to enjoy any kind of longevity, it's wise to base the feature on character as opposed to situation. Character can be adapted to evolving situation, whereas situation cannot always be adapted to evolving character, and may indeed disappear altogether

A strip about a young working girl who has newly entered the work force in an effort to overcome her somewhat financially haphazard background potentially offers a wide variety of possibility for continuing story. A strip about a drive-in movie theatre probably doesn't, especially considering that the number of drive-in movie theatres has dwindled to something less than two dozen in the past decade and the cartoonist could very shortly find himself trying to deal with subject matter that no longer exists.

That's not to say there's anything necessarily wrong with placing your characters inside a drive-in movie theatre. Just make sure your characters--not the theatre--are the focus of the strip.

There is no hard and fast rule as to exactly what kind of character will catch the public's imagination. A quick glance at the comics page of any newspaper will reveal everything from talking animals to semi-sexy girls, from ethnically diverse characters to stereotypical ones, and from gritty curmudgeons to almost hallucinogenic impossibilities.

The selling point of any new comic strip or panel is storytelling. Bearing this in mind, the cartoonist will need to determine exactly what type of character will best allow his story to be told. Whatever character design the cartoonist decides to embrace, he must make certain that the characters are distinct. A female character who reminds the reader of Blondie--just as a brunette instead of as a blonde--isn't likely to find a place on the comic page.

Or anyplace else, for that matter.

The characters must be facile enough for the cartoonist to redraw again and again and again in virtually any position and from any angle. Remember, if your strip is accepted for syndication, you'll be drawing these characters three-hundred and sixty-five days a year, year in and year out. Make certain you're comfortable with the design of your characters.

There are currently six major newspaper syndicates who review comic material-strips and panels--for potential syndication. The submission requirements are pretty much the same for all six.

The cartoonist will need to produce four weeks of daily material, in other words twenty-four daily strips. Most of the syndicates will want to see how you'd handle the Sunday strips, but each has different size requirements for Sundays. It is probably best to use whatever format is in your local Sunday newspaper and produce two Sunday strips, then be prepared to redo them in a preferred format if and when your feature is selected.

Do not send original art for review. The material should be photocopied for submission. A good rule of thumb is to reduce the dailies so that four strips will fit onto a single sheet. The syndicate will want to see how the strip will look when it's reduced to actual printed size, so it's a good idea to reduce them to something approximating actual publication and include this with your submission.

Include a cover letter introducing your feature., but don't try to use the letter as a sales pitch. If the strip doesn't sell itself, no amount of written persuasion is going to make any difference. And, you'll want to include a character breakdown, which details just exactly who's who and what the relationships are. A resume is useful only if you've syndicated a comic feature in the past.

A simple submission package is best. Fancy packaging just makes it more difficult to go review the samples and if reviewing them is perceived as difficult, they'll be ignored. Make sure your name and contact information is printed on every page of the submission.

It's probably a good idea to copyright the work prior to submission. Be sure to note the copyright on each page, as well.

And remember to enclose a self-addressed stamped envelope.

It's been estimated that some eight thousand comic strips and panels are submitted to the syndicates each year for consideration. Of those, less than a dozen will eventually get a shot at appearing on the printed newspaper page and of those less than five will still be up and running after five years. Realistically, most newspapers don't add new strips- they replace old ones. To find success your feature must be good enough to replace a daily favorite of millions of daily newspaper readers.

THE COMIC BOOK & THE GRAPHIC NOVEL

The first American comic book, *Funnies on Parade*, premiered as a giveaway anthology reprinting comic strips from the newspapers in 1934. Needing to dispose of undistributed copies, someone slapped a ten-cent price tag on them and dropped them off at a few newsstands. They rapidly sold out.

The comic book industry was born.

At first comic books were merely reprints of syndicated comic strips from the newspapers, but original material quickly emerged. Thanks to the effects of the Great Depression, it was cheaper for the publishers to purchase new material from aspiring cartoonists than to buy reprint rights from the syndicates.

Many early comic-book creators had no love for the medium. The pay was mediocre, the work grueling and normally the cartoonist worked without acknowledgement. Most worked in comic books with the notion of using the new medium as a stepping stone into the higher paying world of newspaper comic strips. Ironically, the first big comic-book hit was a feature that had been turned down for years by the comic-strip syndicates: Jerry Siegel and Joe Shuster's *Superman*.

The success of Superman led to the proliferation of those costumed characters that have come to be known as Superheroes. By the end of World War II, sales had dried up and by the early fifties the only ones left standing were DC's big three --Superman, Batman and Wonder Woman--and Fawcett's Captain Marvel created by C.C. Beck.

With the decline of superhero genre in the late 1940s, other genres could now take up more of the available newsstand display space. Science fiction lived in titles like

Planet Comics , *Mystery In Space, Space Adventures* and *Weird Science* . Jungle adventure, the type with leggy jungle girls in minuscule leopard-skin bikinis, was another popular genre. It began with the first appearance of *Sheena, Queen of the Jungle* in Jumbo Comics #1 in 1938 and continued in popularity until the mid-1950s.

Archie first appeared in Pep Comics #22 in 1941. Archie contained many of the elements of the romance genre, but the first full-blown romance comic book was *Young Romance* by Jack Kirby and Joe Simon, the same duo who had earlier created *Captain America*.

Pogo by Walt Kelly started out as a comic book series in the first issue of *Animal Comics* in 1940, but by the end of the decade Kelly had achieved the dream of many comic book creators: Pogo became a long-lasting nationwide hit revamped as a newspaper comic strip.

By the mid-1960s, the restrictions placed on content by the Comics Code Authority and the monopoly of corporate-owned characters in comic books were frustrating a new generation of cartoonists who, in keeping with the cultural climate of the times, wanted to explore new methods of expression. At the very least, they longed to create comics that could be read and enjoyed by an adult audience.

Underground comix grew out of the political and cultural disruption of the 1960s and '70s and reflected in graphic terms the issues of the times. Books with titles like *Radical America Komics* , *Corporate Crime Komics*, and the anti-draft *Jesus Meets the Armed Services* sat on shelves in so-called Head Shops alongside books with titles like *Dope* and *Cocaine Comix.*

God Nose by Jaxon is considered by many as the first underground comic.

Gilbert Sheldon's *The Fabulous Furry Freak Brothers* used drugs as its main subject. It looked at American society with a jaded eye and exposed the hypocrisy in the youth culture. As a bonus, it was genuinely hilarious.

Robert Crumb is largely credited with establishing underground comix as a viable commodity. Crumb self-published Zap #1, which became a focus for other graphic artists like Spain Rodriguez and Robert Williams. Crumb went on to produce incredibly twisted, but hilarious, renderings of American Society.

Women cartoonists founded their own comix, such as *Wimmen's Comix, Tits 'n Clits* and *Twisted Sisters*.

The graphic novel is an example of comics evolution. Jules Feiffer released *Passionella* in 1964, arguably the first graphic novel, then released *Tantrum* in 1979. Feiffer had worked as an assistant to Will Eisner, creator of and best known for *The Spirit*, whose own forays into the form include *A Contract With God*.

The Professional Cartoonists' Marketing Guide Page 56

For practical purposes, the primary difference between a comic book and a graphic novel is that the comic book is generally printed for display and distribution during a particular selling period, usually a month, and unsold copies will be removed at the end of that selling period and replaced by the subsequent issue of the title. In other words, July's Anachronistic Man will come off the store shelf the end of the month to make room for the August issue and thereafter will only be available for purchase from those entities specializing in the sale of back-issue comics. Printing the current issue is a one-time affair.

The graphic novel, however, is published with the intent on selling copies for as long as the volume continues to sell. As noted, Pantheon first published Maus in 1986, and the book is still in print and available at most any decent mainstream bookstore.

Comic books are usually marketed specifically to a comic book audience, generally through specialty comic shop retailers, but a graphic novel, depending on the subject matter, is often presented to a much wider audience. Some of the material published under Scholastic's Graphix imprint is marketed and sold directly through chain stores and book retailers, bypassing comic shops entirely.

The comic book, on average, will run anywhere from twenty-two to thirty-two pages of story, with the occasional so-called Special Issue offering a greater number of pages . Graphic novels run the gamut from a usual minimum of sixty-four pages up to several hundred pages of art and story.

Assuming the graphic novel is conceived as a solitary project, not simply a reprinted of previously published material, the cartoonist must make sure that the conception is strong enough to carry this kind of extended storyline.

Consider this scenario: two teenagers are having car trouble while trying to make it home before curfew. Depending on the story conception, this could be a light-hearted six page humor piece in which every solution discovered leads to another hilarious mishap. Or, it could be a sixty-four page suspense tale that finds the teens stumbling on a solitary stretch of country highway barely one-step ahead of a homicidal maniac.

Extending a single scenario humor piece for the length of a graphic novel is bound to become tedious, unless the cartoonist is something of a miracle worker. And, six pages certainly isn't enough to fully explore the ramifications of fleeing in terror through the woods at night. It's important to select the correct format in which to showcase the material the cartoonist intends to present.

The rendering procedure for both the comic book and the graphic novel are virtually identical. The art for both is produced on two-ply smooth (plate) finish Bristol board and drawn to a finished size of ten inches wide by fifteen inches tall, but any proportional size original drawing will work. A one-inch border around the finished is standard, so working on board trimmed to twelve inches by seventeen inches is standard. Bristol board is sold packaged in tablets of fourteen inches by seventeen inches, so a single cut produces the correct size board for a finished comic page.

Few comic book and graphic novel publishers are willing to review a completed project. If the cartoonist's goal is to produce material based on characters owned by an entity other than himself, the "audition" consists of producing six pages of continuity--a sequence that demonstrates not only art ability, but also the cartoonist's storytelling skills. Most comic book publishers produce work using the assembly line model, that is, one person writes the script, another breaks it down into penciled art, another inks those finished pencils, another yet another creator letters the comic pages, then the inked and lettered pages are then handed over to another individual for coloring. If you're submitting for consideration of sliding into that group-assembly process it's important to demonstrate each and every aspect of your skillset.

The cartoonist should photocopy each stage of his audition to showcase his abilities at every stage of the process since very few comics publishers assign the same individual multiple stages of an assigned piece. That said, assuming the cartoonist's skills are adequate and the house style of the content is maintained, some of the humor-oriented comic book publishers are quite happy to look at and subsequently purchase a finished story.

Otherwise, the best the cartoonist can hope for is that his samples will resonate with someone at the publishing company who will file them for future reference or, best scenario, ask for more samples or send a test script for the cartoonist to render.

Comic Conventions serve as the primary vehicle for showcasing samples to Art Directors if one is pursuing piece-work, while complete stories are best submitted directly to the Editorial Offices of the publishing house.

If the cartoonist's goal is to produce material based on characters of his own creation, the submission process still calls for six pages of continuity. Additionally, the cartoonist will need to produce a synopsis of the story line for a potential publisher to review. A cover letter indicating the scale of the project--does the cartoonist see this work as a thirty-two page bi-monthly comic book or as a ninety-six page one-shot graphic novel--is an absolute necessity.

Keep the submission package simple. The work must leap at the editor and leave him hungering for more if there is to be any chance of a publishing partnership. If the editor doesn't see the work isn't extraordinary, the fact that you've earned a Masters degree in Fine Arts, published extensive pro bono cartoon work in your high-school newspaper, or that your mom laughs out loud at every page of your work she's ever taken a look at will do absolutely nothing to encourage publication at this particular venue.

Again, never send original artwork unless and until a specific publisher specifically requests it. The proper submission protocol is to send good quality photocopies for review. Make certain your name, contact information and copyright notification is on each page of the submission.

Electronic submissions attached to email or directing the publisher to a website are often a waste of the cartoonist's time and the hallmark of an amateur. Thanks to the proliferation of malicious online viruses, few if any publishers--or anyone else, for that matter--will risk opening any attachment from someone they don't know.

Compensation varies. If you're working on an established character, some of the better known humor publishers will offer several hundred dollars per page of comic art, depending on exactly what part of the project you're responsible for producing. If you've written, penciled, inked and lettered a complete story that is accepted, compensation can be quite satisfying. Rates tend to increase as the cartoonist continues to produce for a particular publisher.

Comic book publishers who specialize in original comic material, whether the material is to be published in a comic book format as a continuing series or as a graphic novel, are a different matter. The cartoonist is usually paid a royalty on actual sales of the printed material, the same as an author is any other genre of publishing. Some publishers will offer an advance against future royalties and some offer no advance whatsoever. The percentage of the individual purchase price that is to be paid to the author, and when it is to be paid, are part of the negotiated package. The cartoonist needs to make certain that any proffered contract is fully understood before it is signed, and that the contract specifies exactly who owns the intellectual property and who administers any subsidiary rights. The last thing the cartoonist wants to find out after the fact is that the publisher is contractually allowed to sell his creation's movie rights without the creator's agreement and without further compensating said creator.

There are now Literary Agents who specialize in finding appropriate publishers for graphic novels. Depending on content, it may be to the cartoonist's advantage to approach these professionals for representation, but remember not to confuse a Literary

Agent with an Artist's Agent--the two are completely different entities. Most graphic novel publishers are quite willing to review a submitted proposal so unless your material is an appropriate submission to a large publishing house that only reviews material submitted by agents you'll undoubtedly do just as well submitting on your own. It isn't necessary--or even desirable--to pursue a Literary Agent to submit proposed serial material to a comic book publisher.

There's a trend these days for collectives to offer to publish a cartoonist's creation as a means of introducing that cartoonist to the market at large. These collectives offer no compensation, neither a flat fee nor any royalties, instead suggesting that the cartoonist will benefit from the "exposure" and that since the financial investment risk is theirs, the collective should realize a financial return on the work. A buddy of mine some years ago, when approached by such an organization, reminded me that in his home state of Vermont people regularly die from exposure.

Anyone who offers to publish your work without a reasonable financial consideration is a thief. No if, ands or buts. Deal with them accordingly.

And remember, submitting anything to any publisher without enclosing a self-addressed stamped envelope is the equivalent of scrawling the word amateur on every page of your submission.

SELF-PUBLISHING

Some cartoonists have enjoyed a reasonable success self-publishing their own work, either in comic book format or as graphic novels. Dave Sims' *Cerebus* and Terry Moore's *Strangers in Paradise* are good examples of the kind of success possible by establishing a publishing entity and jumping into the perceived chaos of the publishing business.

The upside of self-publishing is that the cartoonist is the one who directly benefits from his creative efforts, negating a sharing of money generated with a separate publisher. The downside is that the cartoonist is the one completely responsible printing, promotion and distribution, and if the product doesn't generate much of a return on investment the cartoonist could well wind up losing money in the process.

There are a number of companies specializing in comic book printing who handle printing for a variety of independent publishers. The cartoonist will likely find local printers with the capacity to print comics, and a variety of companies online with this capacity as well, but finding a printer is not the cartoonist's primary concern.

Distribution is a relatively simple matter, since the only major comics distributor currently operating in the United States is Diamond Distributing. Diamond distributes directly to virtually every comic shop in this country and a number of others. They will review your project to determine if they think it's a viable--read profitable--product for Diamond to handle, and submitting your project for consideration is a much more extensive undertaking that submitting a proposal to an established publisher.

If your proposed publishing project is a serial publication, Diamond will want to see photocopies of at least two fully completed issues before committing its resources. If your project is a one-shot graphic novel, they'll want to see a fully completed copy before reaching a decision. And, they'll want a complete breakdown of your marketing and promotional plan. Diamond will list your product in their wholesale catalog notify you of retailer response to the catalog so you know so you know how many printed copies to order, but without extensive promotion to both retailers and the comics reading consumer your book will get lost between the covers of this telephone directory-sized book. You'll need to spend at least as much on promoting your effort as you plan to spend on printing it

Another avenue to publication is the Print on Demand (POD) option. A number of publishers will access your material to a general audience, then print and ship the book when the customer orders it, then forward a portion of the purchase price to the cartoonist at specified time periods. **CreateSpace**, a division of Amazon, allows the cartoonist to publish his material and list it on every worldwide Amazon sales website. The big advantage of POD publishing is the fact that there is no initial financial investment required, but again, the cartoonist is responsible for promoting the material and without effective promotion sales will be rather thin.

WEBCOMICS

One promotional aspect that offers some possibility of actually generating a return on investment is the Web Comic. The cartoonist reproduces his work, or a portion thereof, online for viewing on the Internet. This exposure, generally free to the site visitor but occasionally available via subscription to the site, introduces the cartoonist's concepts to hopefully an ever-broadening audience and hopefully minimizing the potential loss inherent in paper-copy self-publication. Some web comic sites have actually grown popular enough that their creators are able to partner with advertisers, such as Google, who purchase space on the cartoonist's website. A partnership with a print-on-demand publisher like Cafe Press or Lulu allows the cartoonist to sell merchandise on the site--posters, cups, pens, tee-shirts--and generate income from these items, as well. And, the cartoonist can also sell print copies of his proposed volume via these same print-on-demand companies. The markup or profit percentage will most certainly be less than any profit generated by volume printing, and the cartoonist will most certainly fail at selling these print-on-demand copies to a retailer, but this method does offer publishing possibility with considerably less personal financial investment.

The Professional Cartoonists' Marketing Guide Page 65

Web publication is also a most effective manner of selling the cartoonist's original artwork. Collectors who like the work will certainly consider a purchase, and some will even purchase the work as an investment, hoping you'll turn out to be the next Robert Crumb or Todd McFarland, justifying a resell at many times the original purchase price.

The cartoonist's time is a considerable investment in any self-publishing arena. Not only must the cartoonist coordinate production of the work, printing, shipping and advertising, he must serve as a public relations director to retailers and hopefully newfound fans of his work. And, he must handle all of the accounting functions for his new business.

The self-publisher must still find time to produce more work, building on the audience he's managed to procure. Any number of potentially successful cartoonists have fallen by the wayside because the pressures of self-publishing didn't allow adequate time to write and draw the second issue of what might or even should have been a profitable sequel to the initial effort.

The cartoonist intent on self-publishing must also be intent on riding the convention circuit. The proven most effective method of promoting any comic book or graphic novel is to plant the creator in the middle of tens of thousands comics devotees with money in their pockets and the rest of existence tucked somewhere in the recesses of their minds.

The cartoonist must be realistic about the product he's created. There are certainly exceptions, but if the product isn't perceived by an established comic book publisher as a probable profitable venture, it will probably not prove profitable as an independent publication. True, the larger established publishers will carry a more expensive overhead than the novice publisher, meaning that fewer sales are necessary to generate a profit, but the cartoonist must be aware that profit and viability are sometimes mutually exclusive. A published book can generate a profit, and still not justify the investment in resources and time.

HUMOROUS ILLUSTRATION

Up to this point, we have dealt with those genres of cartooning in which the cartoonist is not only renders the finished version, but is also responsible for conception. The creative process has included both creation and illumination.

Commercial illustration is an area where creation is shared with another individual, indeed sometimes several individuals. Especially in the early stages of his career, the cartoonist will find himself working with an Art Director or a Publisher who has a pretty good idea of what he wants and the cartoonist's responsibility is simply to produce that idea on paper to the client's satisfaction.

In the best case scenario, the cartoonist is given free rein to use his own creative abilities to best illuminate the concept presented, but often the cartoonist's creative sensibilities are of no particular importance to the project. He is perceived as merely a means of getting an existing concept into a visual format and expected to proceed accordingly. The cartoonist who has a fondness for group-think, an infinite amount of patience with the inability of

49

others to make timely decisions and the ability to sidestep the imprint of his own ego can do well in the area of humorous illustration. Those who recognize that they don't play well with others should probably select another sport.

ADVERTISING, BOOKS & MAGAZINES

The purpose of any published illustration is to draw attention to content. Advertising agencies and book and magazine publishers have long used cartoon-type illustration to hook the reader into perusing copy.

Illustrators are generally chosen by sample review. The Art Director selects an appropriate artist from among the many who've contacted him seeking assignment by perusing the filed material he's collected. If the selected illustrator is available and a common ground regarding compensation can be reached, the illustrator is given an assignment to produce the needed work and a deadline schedule for delivery.

Illustrators generally produce work-for-hire, that is, work that will become the sole property of the client. The client will copyright and/or trademark the work as appropriate.

The working process doesn't really vary whether producing work for a magazine or an ad agency. It's the same process as working on assignment for a children's book publisher, assuming that the cartoonist is seeking assignment to produce artwork, not seeking to sell a book he has written and illustrated.

SECURING A CLIENTELE

To secure a clientele, the cartoonist must submit samples of his work that the Art Director can kept on file for reference and possible future assignment.

Good quality reproductions are essential. A good rule of thumb is to reproduce two-to-four illustrations per page, depending on content--if the content is highly detailed and requires a larger space for proper viewing, reproduce two per page, otherwise, four per page is quite acceptable. Three or four pages of reproduced work should be sufficient to demonstrate your style and abilities. As always, contact information and the appropriate copyrights should be noted on each page of your submission. Don't staple the pages together, just paper clip a business card to them.

If you've got published experience, a resume can be helpful. If not, a simple cover letter introducing your work and your availability will suffice. Keep it brief.

Your artwork is what will nudge the Art Director to assign work. Samples may languish in a file cabinet for a couple of year until a project materializes that the AD thinks would be enhanced by your particular drawing style, so if you are going to pursue this market you'll need to make sure you're circulating a volume of sample kits.

Don't include any kind of fee schedule or rate sheet. Most publishers and ad agencies have a payment schedule of their own and at least in the early stages of your cartooning career the choice is pretty much to accept the payment offer or just turn down the assignment because it doesn't pay enough to warrant spending the time producing the work.

GREETING CARDS, POSTERS & PACKAGE DESIGN

The custom of sending greeting cards can be traced back to the ancient Chinese, who exchanged messages of good will to celebrate the New Year, and to the early Egyptians, who conveyed their greetings on papyrus scrolls. The Germans are known to have printed New Year's greetings from woodcuts as early as 1400, and handmade paper Valentines were being exchanged in various parts of Europe in the early to mid-1400s.

The first known published Christmas card appeared in London in 1843, when Sir Henry Cole hired artist John Calcott Horsley to design a holiday card that he could send to his friends and acquaintances. By the 1850s, the greeting card had been transformed from a relatively expensive, handmade and hand-delivered gift to a popular and affordable means of personal communication, due largely to advances in printing and mechanization, as well as the introduction of the postage stamp.

Esther Howland, a young woman from Massachusetts, was the first regular publisher of valentines in the United States. She sold her first handmade valentine in 1849, eventually establishing a successful publishing firm specializing in the elaborately decorated cards, but Louis Prang, a German immigrant who started a small lithographic business near Boston in 1856, is generally credited with the start of the greeting card industry in America. Within ten years of founding his firm, he had perfected the color lithographic process to a point where his reproductions of great paintings surpassed those of other graphic arts craftsmen in both the U.S. and Great Britain. In the early 1870s, Prang began publishing deluxe editions of Christmas cards, which found a ready market in England. In 1875, he introduced the first complete line of Christmas cards to the

American public.

Prang's cards had reached their height of popularity in the early 1890s, when cheap imitative imports began to flood the market, eventually forcing Prang to abandon his greeting card publishing business.

A number of today's leading greeting card publishers were founded in the early 1900s. Most of the cards by these fledgling U.S. publishers bore little relation to Prang's elaborate creations. The expressed sentiment was the predominant element; the illustrated portions were incidental The early 1930s found publishers increasingly adopted the use of color lithography, a move that would propel the U.S. greeting card industry toward continued growth and expansion.

The studio card--a long card with a short punch line-- appeared in the 1950s and firmly establish the popularity of humor in American greeting cards. During the 1980s, alternative cards began to appear, cards not made for a particular holiday or event, but as a more casual reminder of our connections to one another. A quick glance at any retail display rack will confirm the continuing popularity of these non-occasion cards.

The first posters were created in the mid-19th century in France as advertisements for new products. In less than ten years, the use of posters spread from France throughout the rest of Europe. They were used for promotional purposes for theater, and operas shows and major events in Paris and the throughout France. Jules Cheret was the first to give importance to the poster as an artistic image. In 1867, he used the new four-color lithographic process to create a highly stylized form of graphic art that thoroughly integrated text and image. Like Cheret, Henri de Toulouse-Lautrec and Pierre Bonnard designed numerous posters and lithographs during the nineteenth century.

Until World War I, posters were primarily pictorial, depicting artwork, and were sold as merchandise. During the war, this all changed. Posters served warring nations by increasing morale and developing a sense of patriotism and support for the war. They were used to get people to invest in war bonds and government securities. Posters were used to raise funds for the Red Cross and other wartime charities. The use of posters to drum up political support was also a primary use of the medium. The medium was used to best advantage during World War II.

After the war, American posters were primarily a commercial advertising medium, but the 1960s Psychedelic Art movement changed that. Poster artists like Rick Griffin, Victor Moscoso, Stanley Mouse and Alton Kelly, and Wes Wilson helped to revamp the industry. Psychedelic Rock concert posters were inspired by Art Nouveau, Victoriana, Dada and Pop Art. Rich, saturated colors in glaring contrast, elaborately ornate lettering, strongly symmetrical composition, collage elements, and bizarre iconography are all hallmarks of the psychedelic poster art style. Suddenly, the poster was a desirable and often collectible art object.

Today's poster offering run the gamut from fine art reproductions to oversized paintings of animated cartoon characters to obvious comic art designed to both decorate and enchant.

Manufacturers have long known that an enticing image on a product has the potential to greatly enhance sales of that product. Some companies will license popular cartoon imagery to decorate their products, but many will create their own images, sometimes even inventing characters to personalize merchandise. Snap, Crackle and Pop, the three elves adorning the boxes of Kellogg's Rice Krispies are a prime example of this practice.

The cartoonist with an ability to design effectively eye-catching original characters can do very well working with advertising agencies that specialize in Brand Management. The market will also embrace the cartoonist with strong design abilities, that is, the ability to conceive and render any number of items that require cartoon embellishment--items such as paper products (birthday party paper plates and accessories) and packaging (labels and product tags.

Greeting card designs should be packed in batches of six and submitted for review. Publishers often prefer to buy series as opposed to purchasing individual card designs, so it's best to maintain some sense of continuity with each sample package. Copyrighting the designs is optional and if you're submitting to a major publisher probably an unnecessary expense. Make sure to include your name and contact information on each design.

Poster designs are also submitted in batches of six, as well. Collectors often purchase multiple designs from favorite poster artists and publishers prefer the option of having additional material readily available for future release should an artist become suddenly popular. Each poster design should be copyrighted by the artist.

Compensation for greeting cards and posters vary. Some companies will want to purchase the designs outright for a flat fee, buying all rights, while others will negotiate a royalty arrangement based on actual sales. There is nothing wrong with signing away all rights to a design, assuming the cartoonist is comfortable with the compensation offered, and understand that signing away all rights means just that. If your greeting card design winds up as an internationally best-selling poster and you've signed away all rights, well, you'll just have to live with it.

PRODUCT DESIGN

A quick trip through any department, variety or drug store will reveal vast opportunities for the cartoonist with a knack for producing eye-catching character design formatted in a variety of shapes and sizes. Party favors, paper plates and cups, gift wrap, puzzles, coffee mugs, novelty items--all require concept and rendering design.

Product manufacturers and contact sources are best identified using *The Advertiser's Index* and *The Standard Directory of Advertisers.*

Product Designs are also best submitted in multiples of six, again with the cartoonist's contact information and copyright notice clearly marked on each design. Compensation is always negotiated, but some companies will have standard rates of payment they'll want to use as guidelines.

Payment will depend on rights sold, length of contract, the perception by the manufacturer of just how many dollars the design is likely to generate and, quite frankly, the cartoonist's negotiating skills. The cartoonist must understand any and all terms of any contract offered, even if understanding requires review of the contract by a qualified Intellectual Property attorney.

THE CARTOONIST AS PUBLISHER

There is no magic to achieving a lucrative career in the Art Publishing industry, no one particular thing that will guarantee success. Instead, the cartoonist interested in self-publishing his own work must become competent in a variety of different areas and pursue each with unlimited persistence.

The successful self-publishing entrepreneur is a hybrid of artist and businessperson, a merge of two factions often at odds. Like nitroglycerin, the mixture can be perilous. Properly applied, it can explode the restraints that prevent personal accomplishment.

E.B. White is generally regarded as one of the most effective communicators ever to put pen to paper. His prose is direct, expressive and efficient. His masterpiece Charlotte's Web, a favorite with children, and The Elements of Style, a volume on composition that Mr. White shares authorship with William Strunk, Jr., are each in their own right classics. That said, no one would have much cared about Mr. White's verbal functionality if he hadn't had absolutely enchanting things to tell us.

The same simple truth applies to the product you produce. Good marketing habits and effective sales presentation abilities are extraordinary tools, but those tools are completely useless if you're trying to convince a potential customer to invest in a product that is poorly conceived, shoddily rendered, badly reproduced and chaotically packaged.

The first and most important key to success in the Art Publishing Business is the ability to set aside one's artistic ego and consider the rendered art as a viable product. The self-publisher must make a clear determination as to the marketing viability of his or her product because that viability is what determines whether or not a particular design will sell. This isn't meant to imply that the only means to success is to mimic products already on the card shelves, but it does mean that if the new product is considerably different from what the buyer might expect the self-publisher had better be prepared to look a lot longer and a lot harder to find someone to purchase his wares.

From a business perspective, the artist must choose a method of production that allows timely delivery to clients. Production questions should be asked and answered well before a catalog is put in front of a potential customer. The time to decide that hand-painting designs preprinted on cardstock is too time-consuming to allow for a reasonable delivery turn-around time is before the order is placed, not after the order is asked for. A new vendor gets one change to impress a new client with his professionalism, and generally only one chance. Professionals rarely prefer dealing with Amateurs.

The self-publisher needs to explore the total spectrum of product options. Handmade products are usually more expensive and are purchased by collectors, but often a less expensive mass produced reproduction of that design will do quite well in a general retail environment. A dual publishing effort has an enormous potential to increase profit margin, but the effort involved in pursuing a dual market also has the potential to tie up a great deal of the self-publisher's time, both in terms of production and in terms of marketing and distribution. And, if the design will be sold as a reproduction, what method of printing is to be used? Thankfully, printing technology has reached a point where cost is less of an impediment than it once was for the independent publisher.

And, whatever production decisions are instigated, product quality becomes a most important issue. A major selling point of dealing with an independent self-publishing creator, other than the option of acquiring a more unique product, is the quality of that product. As a self-publisher, your name is not only on the original art, it's printed across the reproduced product as well.

PRICING FOR PROFIT, NOT LOSS

It is important to know exactly how much it costs you to produce your individual product. There are variables, depending on the particular formula you choose to determine profit and loss. Your particular formula may include built-in compensation for time spent creating the original product. Or not. It should include promotional costs-after paper supplies and printing costs, promotion will probably be your biggest expense.

Initial success, assuming a viable product, strongly depends on competitive pricing. It isn't necessary to undercut the competition's price, but you don't want a price point considerably above the average, either.

If you're selling directly to consumers, you'll charge a set price. If you're wholesaling to retailers, you'll generally charge 50% of that price. If you're working with a distributor to get your product into store, he'll usually charge 15-20% of the wholesale price.

Individual item cost is the primary factor you'll use in determining most production issues. Spend some time researching product that is similar to your own and determine a reasonable selling price for your own product. Then, begin exploring methods of minimizing your production costs.

The goal of the self-publisher is profit, and the only way to determine profit is to subtract expenses from income. There is nothing more exasperating than having what appears to have been a successful selling year only to have your accountant explain that your profit margin for that fiscal period is almost enough to cover dinner and a movie.

Variety is one of the most important assets available to the self-publishing
entrepreneur. Regardless of whether your focus is selling to individual consumers at craft fairs or retailers or just to anyone with a few extra bucks via the Internet, you'll need a
variety of designs in order to build an effective display. Recommendations vary as to an appropriate number of designs. Individual consumers may not be hesitant about purchasing if you've only got half-a-dozen choices, but retailers want to be assured that if they take a chance on your product, and if that product indeed sells for them, that you're going to be around for them to reorder. The simplest way to moderate those concerns is to have a solid variety of designed product available. You've got to have enough product available to demonstrate to a potential client that you're in it for the long haul and that you are a vendor he can depend upon for ongoing inventory.

Not to mention the fact that mathematically speaking, the more product you have to offer the greater the possibility of selling some of that product.

Okay. You've got a pretty good idea of what your product is going to be. You've figured out what you want to produce and how you want it to look. Now is the time to step back and make certain that the product you have in mind is a product that you not only believe in, but is a product that you can realistically see sitting in a card rack at your local Greeting Card store or in the poster bin at your local Picture Framing shop. It isn't necessary that your subject matter and artistic style possess some mystical universal appeal, but it is necessary that the product you want to sell has a professional appearance--dynamic conception, skilled rendering, quality reproduction and appropriate packaging.

And so, armed with a quality product and a burning desire for financial success, we move to Step Two.

WRITING A TAILORED BUSINESS PLAN

Greeting Card industry estimates show that more than eight billion greeting cards were sold to Americans last year-- which breaks down to about 250 cards sold per second!

Art Reproductions--posters--are selling stronger than ever, bolstered by the Internet and the fact that good imagery requires no foreign language skills to appreciate.

Comic Books are flourishing. There are currently more than four-hundred titles available generating dollars not only from sales of the books themselves, but from licensing projects ranging from action figures to big-budget movie adaptations.

Further good news is that almost half of these products are created and sold by independent creators. If you have a talent for drawing, painting, or cartooning and the gumption to make sure your creative efforts find their way to someplace a potential customer might conceivably find them, there's a better than even chance you can make a success of this business.

As an entrepreneur you'll need to devise a business plan to map the course you'll follow in your day-day-operation. There are two types of business plans.

The first is the financial document assembled in preparation for a business loan conference or to entice investors. This document is best discussed with your accountant and your attorney, and I strongly suggest that if securing a business loan--other than the use of a MasterCard or Visa, which incidentally is the method most often used in America by small business entrepreneurs to finance their business startup--or finding investors is important to you, then by all means secure recommendations from someone you trust and proceed accordingly.

We shall focus on the second variety. The second type of business plan is a personal roadmap you assemble that clearly shows a definite route to follow to reach your destination: success. The bank won't be much interested in this one. It details not only your Product Line, but your Strengths and Weaknesses in areas you wouldn't dare discuss with a financial investor. It clearly delineates your total responsibilities, not only as pertaining to your new Greeting Card Business, but in other seemingly unrelated areas both personal and private. It outlines the criteria by which you'll gauge your progress or lack thereof. It requires an honest consideration of your hopes and dreams and even your talent. Depending on your personal penchant for detail, this can be an exasperatingly complicated document.

Construction of a viable business plan requires you to truthfully answer three questions:

1. What exactly is it that I want?
2. What do I have to do to get what I want?

3. Is doing what I have to do to get what I think I want really worth the trouble?

I sincerely belief the reason most small businesses fail is because the entrepreneur neglected full consideration of Question Number Three.

As your own boss, you have total control over what you want to create. No guidelines to adhere to, no editor to follow, and no bureaucracy to go along with, but there is one important drawback: you are not focused solely on the creation aspect. You need to take care of the supply chain, production, financing, marketing, selling, bookkeeping and administrative tasks. This process is generally exhilarating to the Entrepreneur and exasperating to the Artist. Most creative people don't decide to purse a creative career so they can spend half their time involved in administrative, production and promotional tasks. It's important to strike a balance between the two. You want to schedule your activity so that you're as productive as possible on the business end without dampening your enthusiasm for the creative process.

A recent survey suggested that even the most productive people working in a corporate office are actively involved in actually doing their job a little less than five hours a day no matter how many hours they spend in the office. The rest of the day is interruptions, chit-chat, personal business and breaks. If you're determined to successfully combine a personal business operation with your creative endeavors, you need to learn how to focus on what's truly productive and ignore the chatter.

In order to write an effective individualized business plan, you have to decide exactly what your initial product offering will be. You can amend that product later, but you have to have one to start with. Your concerns will be unique to your situation and as such a cookie cutter business plan will do you little to no good. Indeed, it may actually hurt you in the long run.

There are a wide variety of variables that must be included to make your plan a valid one. Production costs will vary thanks to different design factors. If your products are handmade, you're dealing with the cost of raw materials. If your products are to be reproduced, you're dealing with the cost of raw materials as well as the cost of whatever printing method you decide upon. If you decide on commercial printing, you'll need to include shipping and possible storage consideration. You'll need to stock the proper sized envelopes and mailing boxes. If you've decided your product would do well in a festival environment and decided to play the street fair circuit, you'll need display racks, a table and comfortable portable chair. You'll also need a dependable method of transportation to cart these things to the affair

You'll need to think about financing. Starting an art publishing business is considerably less expensive than buying a McDonald's franchise and a lot less fattening, but there are expenses involved and it will take time to begin generating any dollar volume, much less any that could conceivably be considered profit--which means you'll need to think about living expenses and devise some method of supporting yourself while you're building your business.

And, you'll need to sketch out both a short-range and a long-range plan of action. What shape do you want your business to be in six months from now? A year from now? Three years from now?

What are you prepared to do to get it there? And what are you not prepared to do?

The only justification for being in business is to generate profit. You may produce art to satisfy your creative urges, but the moment you've signed your name to the piece it must be viewed as a product, and exchanging that product for cold, hard cash is the only rationale for enduring the frustration that comes with the daily operation of any business entity. Well, that and avoiding the necessity of a part-time career in food service.

There is a certain charm connected to doing business directly with the artist. It is perceived that there is more certainty in doing business with a businessperson. Learn to separate the creative aspect of your personality from the entrepreneurial side of your personality. Don't abandon either one of them, just learn when to show which and when to show a little of both.

Chances are you became a cartoonist because the idea of creation fascinated you. Some inwardly driven force compelled you to pick up a pencil or a brush or a camera or paper and scraps of glue and apply your most concentrated efforts.

And every cartoonist I've ever spoken with wants to sell enough of his work to support him or herself. It's only reasonable to hope to make a living doing the thing you love the most.

Cartoonists tend to speak in terms of inspiration when it comes to creation. That's all well and good, but there's a little voice that squeaks between my ears insisting that inspiration is little more than unfocused observation. If you're going to assume the responsibility for proactively selling enough of your work to allow you to devote your full efforts to producing more of it, it's important to remember that the day comes and the day goes and those who wait for inspiration to spur them into action are generally found game shows on one of the television cable networks. Good time management is of the utmost importance. Your working time must be scheduled. Yes, as a self-employed, budding business mogul you certainly have the final say in determining just how flexible you'll be with the time you have available, but the business aspect of your dual career is at least as important as the creative aspect and if you're anything like the rest of us, especially those of us with a creative bent, it's very easy to let the time you meant to spend on business slip away while you toil away on the next masterpiece. There's the suggestion that you can plan to win or you can plan to fail; not planning or failing to follow your plan is simply planning to fail.

Dedicate a specific period of time each day to just the business aspect of your career. In the beginning, you'll need time to assemble promotional packages and make telephone calls. As those efforts result in orders, you'll need time to reproduce, package and ship them, but you'll still need the time to handle promotion. As you begin to see more results from your promotional activity--and you will see results if you're both consistent and persistent--you'll need even more time to get the product out to your customers. With luck, you'll reach a point where your business efforts are eating up so much of your time you begin to worry about the amount of creation time you have available. At that point, you'll hopefully be able to afford to hire someone to handle monotonous little details--like folding cards and packaging promotional material--that don't absolutely require your hands-on expertise.

Someone once defined an entrepreneur as someone willing to work eighty hours a week for himself so he didn't have to work forty hours a week for someone else. The upside of it is that the entrepreneur is the one who benefits financially from his efforts.

No one believes in a product that has no value, not even the person who created it. If you believe in your product and you believe in your talent, the very least you can do is give yourself the opportunity to benefit financially from your talents.

Success in any endeavor that involves selling a product requires recognition of the numbers factor. The more people who see your product, the greater the chances are of finding someone who wishes to purchase your product. Statistically, the best chance for continuing financial success is getting your product into the retail stores. It doesn't matter whether you're selling an original handmade product or a quality reproduction, you've got a much better chance of exposing your work to the greatest number of people in an atmosphere that is more exclusively conducive to buying than any other venue. Street Fairs and Craft Shows can certainly result in additional income, and are a terrific promotional gambit, but a retail environment showcases your product day in and day out. And, since that retail environment is your best bet, you'll want to put your product into as many retail stores as possible.

You'll want to pursue Distributors to handle your product, but you don't necessarily want to wait for them to produce sales. You may also find that Distributors are more interested in carrying a product that has already proven its viability in the marketplace, so if you've got product in some stores you'll having an easier time signing a Distributor.

At a minimum, your promotional efforts should include ten sales packages mailed to retailers each and every week. That means you'll schedule ten follow-up sales calls for the following week.

At a minimum, your promotional efforts should include five sales packages mailed to distributors each and every week. That means you'll schedule an additional five follow-up sales calls for the following week.

You should contact retailers who become customers once a month to introduce new product and solicit new orders.

Get used to the concept of rejection. It isn't personal and it isn't even necessarily a reaction to the quality of the work your produce. Retailers and distributors are in business to generate profit and both will readily acquire whatever new product they think will appeal to their customer base. It may just be that your product isn't seen as something their existing customers will embrace.

Or, they just might not like your stuff. People are human and knee-jerk reactions are common. That's okay, too. If people didn't have different preferences the opportunity for success in the art publishing business would be non-existent.

Somewhere in that crowd of potential customers out there are the ones who will find your particular product enchanting, will place an initial order, display your product to best advantage and reorder when those are gone. The trick is to identify them, and the only way to do it is pick a starting spot in the crowd and start asking.

Every one of them who tells you *NO* brings you one step closer to finding the ones you're looking for. The more people you ask every day, the more quickly you'll find them.

THE CARTOONIST AND THE COMPUTER

There are two methods of web site promotion: Direct and Indirect.

Direct Promotion refers to making the best use of those established procedures designed to help the seeker readily identify and locate those sites appropriate for his needs, i.e., Search Engines and Referral Sites.

The most effective tool in the Direct Promotion of a website is the Search Engine. Search Engines gather information on existing web sites by either scanning a list of keywords supplied by the Web Master at the time of registration or by scanning the words on the first page of the web site itself. It is, therefore, of utmost importance to post copy on the first page of your site that states in no uncertain terms who you are and what you do.

Registering your site with a Search Engine is a relatively quick process. Simply go the main page of the Search Engine and look for the icon that says something to the effect of "Register a Site". Click on the icon and follow the instructions. Some Search Engines will offer a "Priority" for a fee, either quicker consideration of your site for inclusion or sometimes a promise to list your site sooner when a query is posted rather than later in the list. You'll have to make your own determination as to whether or not you wish to spend the money, but just registering your site without a financial investment is usually appropriate. If you find yourself registering with a Search Engine that demands a registration fee, back out immediately.

If you're selling product from your website, organize the site into two sections: a portfolio section and a catalog section. Visitors who are considering contracting you for commercial services aren't generally interested in wading through the thirty poster images you're pushing. In fact, the notion that you've referred an art director to a selling catalog is could be enough to give him second thoughts about contacting you for future work.

If you're going to sell from your site, make it easy for your customers to buy. If the only payment method you're setting up is to print out and order form and mail a check, you're going to lose a lot of potential customers. If product variety warrants, set up an online shopping cart, but at the very least insert a PayPal icon for each item. PayPal also allows buyers to make purchases from your site using Credit Cards.

If you are selling product directly to consumers on the site, consumers should be directed to their own section. If you're selling wholesale on the site, it's a good idea to have a separate wholesale section. Post a link on the first page of your site that will take the wholesaler to where he needs to be, just as you posted a link that will carry the art director to a simple portfolio section.

A printable order form is a must, even if you're set up for online ordering. Give your customers the option of ordering in whatever manner is comfortable for them.

Clearly state minimum order requirements. Tell your customers approximately how long they'll have to wait for merchandise, retail or wholesale, and make certain the orders go out in a timely fashion.

If you're interested in talking with distributing firms, convey that information on a separate and distinct page from the other pages.

Imagine yourself standing inside a retail store at a greeting card display. If inflated promotional objects popped out at you every time you attempted to remove a card from the rack for consideration or if the rack began to spin every time you reached for a card, you'd probably leave.

So will most web surfers. The idea is to make it as easy as possible for the potential customer to peruse your samples. Remember, he isn't there because he's looking to be impressed with your marvelous ability to create a website. Don't let the web site become so annoying that actually looking at your artwork is the last thing a visitor would consider.

It's been estimated that you've got about four seconds to capture a web surfer's attention--if you're lucky. Every loading delay you build into your site increases the possibility that he'll be gone before the entire site is visible. Don't assume most visitors have high-speed internet access.

SPAM is an annoying fact of life. Most of us utilize some sort of screening software to sort out those unwanted solicitations and they are deleted without being read. It might be okay to send a one-time email invitation to visit your web site to a party you don't know, but unless you can do it in multiples of hundreds of thousands your return on the effort is bound to be negligible. You'll realize a much better return by offering an emailing list on your site so visitors who already have an interest in what you have to offer know when to return to take a look at your updated products.

Print advertising has proven extraordinarily ineffective as a means of securing visitors to your website, not to mention expensive. The simple truth is that people who chance upon your site while they are online are much more likely to visit than people who find your URL in a magazine and have to write it down and remember to punch in the web address the next time they venture online.

Indirect Promotion refers to making the best use of secondary functions to help the seeker identify and locate those sites appropriate for his needs. Your greeting cards or posters are products and their primary function is to be sold, but an effective secondary function is as a promotional beacon, a beacon lit by the placement of your web address on the back of each individual card or listed in small type at the bottom of your poster. Someone who has already purchased a reproduction of your art is likely to consider a future purchase and a quick referral to your online catalog is a good way to make that next purchase an easy thing to do.

Social media is a primary example of Indirect Promotion. Facebook, Twitter and all the rest are good and inexpensive ways to identify and inform folks who may have an interest in your product. You make photo cards with horses on them? Common sense suggests that an Equestrian Chat Group might have a few members who'd be interested in buying from you. Or a Rodeo Group. Or a group of Horse Racing Enthusiasts. SPAMMING the members of a chat group isn't appropriate, but an introductory notice on the Message Board with a subdued invitation to visit your website for a look at what you do certainly is.

A variety of online companies seek to partner with creators. Companies such as Red Bubble and Cafe Press offer the opportunity to place your designs on products they produce and sell for a commission through their own web site. While a real opportunity for profit to the creator might be dubious, most of these companies offer a free web page to showcase your image on their products and will allow you to post a link to your web site on that page. And, there is usually no cost to set up a product line.

On occasion, you'll receive a request to use one or more of your images on someone else's website. These kinds of requests generally come from non-commercial sites from someone who became enchanted with your work. Consider allowing the use of your work in exchange for credit and a link back to your web site listed with the image.

Take advantage of every no-cost online opportunity to post a referral to your web site.

Finally, a few observations that should prove useful:

Every effort should be made to make your visitors want to revisit your site. Change the content every 30 days or so, even if all you do is to move everything around for a different aesthetic. Your visitor won't remember everything that was on the site anyway, but he will generally notice if it doesn't look like the site has been changed.

Get that Visitor Counter off of your site! A new visitor who finds out he's the thirty-fourth one to hit your site may figure there must be nothing there worthwhile or you'd be getting more traffic. Believe me, he won't wait for the rest of the page to load. An invisible counter you can access from behind the site will tell you how much traffic you're getting. Those numbers are nobody's business but your own.

Establish a Visitor's Log and offer a signup block for an Email List. People who sign your log do so because your product appeals to them. Most people won't take the time to sign up if they don't think they might have a future need for your product. In fact, people who'll voluntarily signup for even more email deposited into their Inbox probably have a definite thought in mind for the future. Email a "Thank You" to everybody who signs the log or signs up for the mailing list--you can compose a standard response and have the message sent automatically.

Don't make the Visitor's Log available for public viewing. In the first place, some of your more ambitious competitors are perusing Visitor's Logs to determine who might be in the market for an introductory email invitation, and second, you don't want a visitor leaving your site having just read a nasty comment posted by some disgruntled fifteen-year-old kid who chose your venue to verbally vent his own frustrations.

Promoting yourself and your product on the Internet requires the same dedication and attention as promoting the physical product in the local market. The difference is that the Internet allows access to customers worldwide and the biggest promotional cost is time. Your website is one of the most effective--and inexpensive--sales and marketing tools at your disposal. It gives you the opportunity to put your skills and the results of those skills in front of everyone in the world that has access to a computer, and all without print cost.

Your website should certainly contain every appropriate image you have available. Those images should be easy to access without a lot of splashy animation involved in the web page setup to aggravate those potential customers who find their way to your site. The concentration span of the modern consumer is extremely short--this isn't meant as an insult, but rather an observational statement of fact--and if your visitor has to wait longer than a few seconds for your page to load, chances are that he won't.

Your URL should be listed on every piece of business paraphernalia associated with your business: business cards, promotional pieces, and definitely on your letterhead.

COPYRIGHT, TRADEMARK & WORK-FOR-HIRE

The cartoonist will want to make certain ownership of any work produced is clearly established and that the work is protected from being used without the cartoonist's permission.

A copyright protects an original artistic or literary work.

Copyright is a form of protection provided by the laws of the United States to the authors or creators of original works, including literary, dramatic, musical, artistic, and certain other intellectual works. A completed work is automatically copyrighted, but that copyright must be registered to insure ownership and legal protection. This protection is available to both published and unpublished works. The Copyright Act gives the owner of the copyright the exclusive right to do and to authorize others to do the following:

To reproduce the work

"To prepare derivative works based upon the work

To distribute copies of the work to the public by sale or transfer of ownership, or by rental, lease, or lending

To display the copyrighted work publicly

It is illegal for anyone to violate any of the rights provided by the copyright law to the owner of copyright, meaning that copyrighted material cannot be used without the permission of the copyright owner. There are, however, limitations on these rights. In some cases, these limitations are specified exemptions from copyright liability. One major limitation is the doctrine of "fair use". In other instances, the limitation takes the form of a "compulsory license" under which certain limited uses of copyrighted works are permitted upon payment of specified royalties and compliance with statutory conditions.

Copyright issues can become increasingly complicated and this book isn't designed to be a legal referendum on the issue. For further information about the limitations of any of these rights, consult the copyright law or write to the Copyright Office. A bulk of information--and the website for copyright filing--is accessible at

http://www.copyright.gov/

Artwork is usually copyrighted using Form VA. It is permissible to copyright more than one image per form. Each filed form necessitates a filing fee, so copyrighting multiple images on the same form can result in an immediate savings. The work would be copyrighted as a compilation using the title, for example, *Douglas Ready's Studio Work, September 2016-August 2017*. Be aware, however, that the courts have dictated that infringement of a copyrighted work might require compensation to the copyright holder based on that portion of the work used without the creator's permission--in other words, if you've filed ten images on the same copyright form and only one of them is the victim infringement, the compensation due could be determined at ten percent (10%) of the amount you would have recovered if the image had been copyright separately.

Copyrighted work should be marked with the proper copyright notice. The notice consists of three parts: (1) either the symbol © (preferred because it also meets the requirements of the Universal Copyright Convention), the word Copyright or the abbreviation Copr.: (2) the year of first publication and (3) the name of the copyright owner. A proper copyright notice looks like this:

©2017 Douglas Ready

Copyrighted work should always be displayed with the proper copyright notice. Reproductions of the original image should always note the registered copyright. The copyright notice informs the viewer that all rights pertaining to use and reproduction of the image are retained by and reserved to the copyright owner. If there is no visible copyright notice, the viewer may well assume the image is in the Public Domain, i.e., for all intents and purposes belongs to no one in particular and its use is fair game. A lack of a posted copyright notice is generally a viable defense for copyright infringement.

All work the cartoonist intends to retain ownership of should be copyrighted.

A **Work for Hire** describes a situation where the artist is retained to create a specific piece of work that will upon completion be owned in its entirety by another party. The artist's compensation is dependent upon transfer of ownership and all rights to the artwork to that party--in other words the artist is paid a one-time fee and waives any future claim to the work, including any say in the use of the imagery on subsidiary products, and residuals or commissions on that subsidiary usage. The party that retained the artist owns the image lock, stock and barrel and can do with it as they darn well please. The client will generally register the copyright under these circumstances.

A **Trademark** is a word, phrase, symbol or design, or a combination of words, phrases that identifies and distinguishes the source of the goods or products of one party from those of others. A service mark is the same as a trademark, except that it identifies and distinguishes the source of a service rather than a product.

You can establish rights in a mark based on legitimate use of the mark. However, owning a federal trademark registration on the Principal Register provides several advantages, e.g., constructive notice to the public of the registrant's claim of ownership of the mark; a legal presumption of the registrant's ownership of the mark and the registrant's exclusive right to use the mark nationwide on or in connection with the goods and/or services listed in the registration; the ability to bring an action concerning the mark in federal court; the use of the U.S registration as a basis to obtain registration in foreign countries; and the ability to file the U.S. registration with the U.S. Customs Service to prevent importation of infringing foreign goods.

Any time you claim rights in a mark, you may use the "TM" (trademark) or "SM" (service mark) designation to alert the public to your claim, regardless of whether you have filed an application with the United States Patent and Trademark Office (a patent protects an invention). However, you may use the federal registration symbol "®" only after the USPTO actually registers a mark, and not while an application is pending. You can file your application directly over the Internet using the Trademark Electronic Application System (TEAS) available at

http://www.uspto.gov/teas/index.html

LICENSING

There are those instances when the artist creates an image solely of his own volition and decides to exploit that image in multiple venues for financial gain. Fabrics, party items such as paper plates, cups and napkins, a wide range of collectables, novelty items, tee-shirts, wrist watches--all depend on eye-catching graphic enhancement, read pretty picture, to help influence the consumer decision to purchase. Some cartoon designs are easily adapted as product designs for items such as toys, statuettes, puzzles, posters, and even fine art prints. Assigning reproduction rights for your imagery to companies involved in product manufacturing-- as opposed to selling the company the design outright--is called Licensing.

Licensing allows you to fully exploit the imagery you've created, allowing more opportunity for additional income from that imagery without the need to launch an additional product line that you must manufacture and promote. You retain ownership of the image, but allow other companies to reproduce it on a particular product during a specified time frame in exchange for monetary compensation.

Think of licensing as renting your image for use on a specific product for a specified period of time. The company is responsible for manufacturing, promoting and selling the finished product. Approaching a potential licensing client is much the same as approaching an Art Director to secure a free-lance assignment. The biggest difference is that in approaching a potential licensing client your objective is to sell him on using an image you've already produced as opposed to securing an assignment to produce work he might have in mind. However, it isn't unusual to approach a potential licensing client who isn't interested in the imagery you're shopping, but appreciates your rendering style and asks if you'd be interested in doing free-lance work design for his company. In this instance, the company will generally consider all assignments a Work for Hire and will own the art and all rights from the moment you're compensated. The decision to accept work in this capacity as a free-lancer or not is a matter of personal choice.

The easiest way to identify potential licensing clients is to stroll through a retail store and take a look at what's on the shelf. If, for example, you think your designs would work well as puzzles, take a look at the puzzles you find in the stores and determine which puzzle manufacturers might use the kind of imagery you produce. Most every company has its specialty and puzzle manufacturers specializing in cartoon character puzzles for small children will usually have little interest in acquiring reproduction rights to a Fine Art quality photograph.

Licensing proposals are usually directed to either the Art Director or the New Product Development Director (exact titles vary, but they're close enough to jump out you), and these folks are easily identified by checking the company listing in the *Advertiser's Index*, a volume that list contact information of every company in the United States that spends more than $50,000 annually in advertising. The book is expensive, but the Business Section of most libraries will have a copy. Alternately, look up the company online and telephone to ask to whose attention Licensing Proposals should be directed.

The proposal should contain a letter stating your intent and a copy of the imagery you're proposing for consideration. You'll want to enclose a copy of six different images per proposal package. Making several proposals while you've got a prospect's attention is just good business sense. It's sometimes a good idea to also enclose a reformatted version of an image, especially if you're proposing its use on a product with a specific shape, i.e., if you think your rectangular image would do well on a paper plate, it's probably a good idea to trim that image into a circle before submission. Reformatting helps make visualization for the Art Director or the New Product Development Director a much easier process.

Follow up the proposal package in the same manner you'd follow up any sample package you've mailed to an Art Director. Enclose a self-addressed stamped envelope for the return of your samples in the event of non-interest.

So, let's assume you've connected with a company that's interested in using your art for their products. They'll want you to read and sign a legal agreement that gives them the right to use your art--and perhaps even a bit more that you're not prepared for.

Licensing your imagery is a legal issue. Many artists make mistakes that would have been completely avoidable if they had understood a few basic terms or if they had known how to read a licensing agreement. There are many holes that an artist can step into on the In most cases, the company will offer you their Licensing Agreement. It's important to fully read and understand the contract before you sign it, if for no other reason to make certain that you're licensing your imagery and not selling it outright.

There's nothing wrong with selling all reproduction rights to an image as long as you're satisfied with the dollar compensation you receive and understand that you no longer own the image and have no right to use it. The problem kicks in when you're talking about licensing and the company is talking about purchasing This difference in understanding often becomes apparent when their Assignment of Rights contract is presented.

You can get into trouble when the company has you sign an agreement which gives them all reproduction rights, now and in the future, to one of your images. That means that they--not you--own the art. Since they own your art they can use it for anything they want, resell it to another company, or license it to other companies for other uses for the next hundred years or so and you legally have absolutely no say in the matter.

You'll never make another cent from that image.

Owning all reproduction rights is generally what a company means when they say they "buy all rights". This kind of arrangement works for illustrators and photographers who work on assignment and know full well that once they're paid by the client they'll never be able to use the art again. These folks generally understand what they're getting into when they sign a release. The problems kick in when an artist doesn't know what he or she is getting into.

The artist cannot rely on the friendliness of the people at the company and their verbal assurances. You certainly want an amiable working relationship with a client, but any verbal statement is negated once the contract is signed.

If you have any questions about the content of the contract and your rights and obligations once you've signed it, speak to an attorney. When they're in law school, attorneys learn about contracts and contract law, but without specific application to the fields of art and licensing. Make certain the attorney you're paying to review the contract has the necessary experience to recognize how certain key provisions of the agreement can affect your future ability to market your work.

The artist himself--and I cannot stress this enough-- must read every line in the agreement himself and make sure he understands it. If you find that there are sections or sentences that aren't written clearly, don't say what you want, take away a bit more of your rights than you feel you want to give or if any of it seems confusing or contradictory, have the company rewrite it in plain English.

These are just a few of the examples of the kinds of things that companies insert into their contracts that the artist should be wary of:

1. The company gains the copyright for any of your pieces of art.

2. The company gains full and complete reproduction rights to any of your art.

3. The company gains the right to sublicense your art to other companies without your having to approve and sign each specific sublicensing agreement.

4. The company gains full ownership of your original works of art as part of the licensing agreement.

If the company isn't willing to rewrite the licensing contract to address these issues, then you may just want to think twice about what you're getting yourself into.

Don't let this kind of thing stop you from promoting your art for license. Most companies are reputable and most contracts are completely understandable by the average person. Just make sure you read every word, and know what it means.

Licensing contracts should always specify the length of time the license is for. And, it should address several issues that will present themselves at the end of the contract's term.

Reversionary rights are common in most license agreements, especially if the license has a fixed term of several years. Look for provisions entitled "Termination," "Term," "Reversion," "Grant of Rights," "Exploitation," or "Commercialization" to find reversionary rules. But be careful if a license agreement says it is "perpetual" or lasts "for the life of the copyright" or has similar language. There may not be any reversionary language and the agreement may not deal with the issue at all. This type of agreement would probably amount to an assignment of your rights, rather than a term of license.

When you locate language in a license agreement that describes a reversion, you need to determine the circumstances in which your rights would revert to you --in other words, what has to happen in order for you to get the rights back. Ideally, you would want the rights to revert in the event that (1) the agreement terminates, (2) the company stops selling your work for a fixed period of time, (3) the company doesn't start selling your product by a certain date, or (4) the company materially breaches the agreement. It's pointless asking for reversion in the event that the company goes bankrupt because federal law usually prevents that from happening.

Foreign licensing of your artwork can also be lucrative, but it raises a number of additional concerns. When you allow a foreign company to license and sell your artwork as merchandise, the most important issue that arises has to do with people, not the contract. You can hire the world's most gifted lawyer to create a foreign licensing agreement, but if the other party is somewhat less than honest, or just inept, it doesn't matter what's printed on the agreement. You'll have to chase them into court in a foreign country and, assuming you win, you still have to collect your judgment before the licensee goes bankrupt or otherwise closes his doors. When considering foreign licensing, start by asking two questions:

1. Has this company or person ever licensed artwork from a U.S. artist before?

Don't be the first U.S. artist to deal with a foreign licensee. If a company has no experience with American licensors, you should have a strong reason to proceed with them, say, for example, the principals of the company are experienced in international licensing, although the company itself is new.

2. If the company has licensed artwork from U.S. artists, who are they and how can you contact them?

Get the names and contact info for all of the artists who license with the foreign company, not just those recommended by the company. Find out whether those artists are satisfied with the company's quality, accounting, and general responsiveness.

Assuming you're satisfied that the company is reliable, you'll either be given a standard licensing agreement or you'll have to furnish one. In the case of foreign licenses, you're better off providing your own.

These are some of the important foreign licensing issues to keep in mind:

1. ***Approval of licensed goods***. It is reasonable to demand that copies of your licensed work be sent to you on a regular basis for approval. This offers you some assurance of consistency and quality for your work.

2. ***Royalties and accounting***. Payment of royalties from a foreign licensee can get tricky, especially when you consider issues like currency conversion rates, how the money will be paid, and what taxes may be applied against your sales or
royalties. Before signing the license, inquire into national or local taxes that may apply. It's wise to include an audit provision which allows you to inspect the foreign licensee's books.

3. ***Jurisdiction***. Jurisdiction is the power of a court to bind the parties by its decision. Unless the company does substantial business in the states, the only way to get a foreign licensee into a U.S. court is to include a provision in the license agreement that requires the licensee to consent to U.S. jurisdiction.

4. ***Choice of law***. Every country--and every state--has laws as to how contracts are interpreted. The licensee will want the disputes to be resolved under the laws of its country. Try to include in your agreement that disputes will be resolved
under U.S. law for copyright purposes and the laws of your state when it comes to   contract issues.

5. ***Arbitration***. Using arbitration, the parties hire a neutral arbitrator to evaluate
the dispute and make a determination instead of filing a lawsuit. You'll almost always benefit by agreeing to have disputes arbitrated and inserting this into your agreement. If possible, your agreement should award attorney fees to the victor in the arbitration.

6. *Foreign registrations*. If your works are protected by U.S. intellectual property laws like copyright, you should determine whether it's worth your while to obtain foreign copyright in the countries where your work is being manufactured or distributed. You may be able to require that the licensee handle these administrative tasks as part of the license.

Until you've gone through the licensing process enough times to feel completely comfortable, consult a qualified attorney in every licensing instance. Failure to fully understand a legal agreement can result in a signed contract that obligates you to things you'd normally never even consider.

Contracts aside, it's important that you're comfortable with the people you're dealing with at the company, particularly if you're going to be responsible for producing variations on the image to customize its use, but don't allow a feeling of camaraderie to interfere with your ability to make prudent decisions. If in doubt, don't do the deal. Don't let your desire to earn royalties overcome your common sense.

Whether pursuing an outright sale or whether pursuing licensing opportunities, many cartoonists set themselves up for failure in one of two ways: they either approach a potential client with inappropriate material, or they simply don't approach enough potential clients. Both circumstances can be overcome if the cartoonist strongly believes in himself and in the work he produces and is willing to buckle down do what needs to be done.

BUSINESS LICENSES, TAXES & OTHER VARIOUS & SUNDRY ISSUES GUARANTEED TO CAUSE SLEEPLESS NIGHTS

Every state or province and virtually every locale requires a license to operate a business. Specific requirements and statutes vary from place to place, but what it all boils down to is that the municipality in which you live is going to charge you for the privilege of conducting business inside its borders.

Depending on the scope of your business operation, there are other fees you might need to concern yourself with. If you're selling retail, you may need to collect sales tax. If you're just selling wholesale, you probably won't need to worry about it, but--again, depending on where you're located--you might still be liable for filing that particular tax paperwork every year to inform them you didn't collect any sales tax monies.

Every state and municipality has an office dedicated to helping you understand just exactly what your obligations and responsibilities are. They've also got an office dedicated to rounding up those folks who don't make the effort.

The Internal Revenue Service offers a free seminar to those people who are considering forming a small business. It deals with a number of issues that probably wouldn't occur to anyone who has never had to file a Federal Tax Return that included self-generated income.

Make sure you contact your local tax office, your state tax office and the IRS before you actually begin presenting your product for sale. Believe it or not, they really are there to help, and they actually want you to be successful. Very successful. The more successful you are, the more taxes they're allowed to collect.

USING THE BUSINESS LICENSE TO BEST ADVANTAGE

Many of us tend to view a Business License solely as a legal obligation we must pay. Used properly, possessing a license can actually increase your profitability.

Generally speaking, supplies bought for use in production of products that will be presented for sale are non-taxable, even when bought at the retail level. You'll have to show your license and the store will probably have you sign a Reseller Statement certifying your purchase is just that, but in Washington State the sales tax is right at 10%- saving $10 for every $100 I spend on supplies makes it worthwhile to take a moment and fill out the paperwork. And, a great many retailers will offer a professional discount if they've seen your license.

KEEPING THOSE RECORDS UP TO DATE

The fledgling small business person usually gets into trouble because he or she failed to document those things that directly influence the bottom line. Possession of a business license announces your serious intent to tax authorities. You're now responsible for state and federal income taxes, any local income taxes, sales taxes that must be collected on retail sales and forwarded to the state, and any additional fees for services that might not readily be apparent.

On a more positive note, many of the costs of operating a business are tax deductible, meaning those costs are deducted from your income and you are only taxed on the difference between the two.   In addition to expenses for supplies and postage, if you're working out of your home a portion of your rent or mortgage and your utilities is probably now tax deductible as a business expense. Should you decide to incorporate, things like Health Insurance and other company-paid benefits may be deductible.

Requirements vary from state to state, as well as from circumstance to circumstance, , so it's best to talk with a tax professional. The idea is to pay every single cent of the taxes you owe, but not a penny more, and a tax professional is in a much better position to insure that you take advantage of every deduction.

Incidentally, the tax professional's fee is also deductible.

A FINAL WORD

There is no magic involved in achieving a successful, sustained career in the field of cartooning. Honing one's skills, exploring a variety of genres and venues, and careful pairing of ability and product, and perseverence is the key.

After that, it's just a matter of doing the very best work you can do and making sure that only your very best efforts leave the studio.

...and make sure a lot of work leaves the studio.

I wish you well.

T

TOOLS OF THE TRADE

Following are sample contracts the cartoonist may find useful.

These are provided solely as examples. Any contract should be reviewed by a competent attorney before the cartoonist's signature binds him or her to a legally enforceable agreement.

Sample Bill of Sale for Original Art

Date:_____

Title:

_____

Sold
to:_____
Address:

_____

Telephone & Email:_____

    Price: $ _____

    Shipping: $ _____

    Total: $ _____

Unless otherwise specifically indicated, all works herein are originals executed by the artist and are certified to be free from defects due to faulty craftsmanship or faulty materials for a period of twelve months from the date of sale. If flaws should appear during this period and be due to such causes, said works shall be subject to repair or replacement at the option of the seller. Buyer is cautioned, however, that the seller cannot be responsible for fading, cracking, and other damage to the work caused by improvident exposure to sunlight and weather.

All shipments are fully insured by the shipper against damage or loss. If works are not received in good condition, please notify the seller within ten days of receipt. All shipments will be transferred via freight collect unless prepaid by the buyer. Crating methods and charges are per art object freight company standard procedures and rates.

The original works described herein are copyrighted by the artist. The sale of such copyrighted work does not include the sale of rights to reproduction in any form unless specifically granted in writing by the artist.

Sample Work-For-Hire Agreement

This is an agreement between (Name) _____of (Company Name) _____,hereinafter referred to as the Client and (Artist's Name) _____, hereinafter referred to as the Artist, for the creation and transfer of the Work. All right and liabilities of either party in the work shall be governed by this agreement.

1. Artist will create _____ artworks for (Name of Project).

2. Artist shall submit the artworks in finished form no later than (Date).

3. Client will pay the artist the sum of $_____ for each artwork, to be paid

one-half upon delivery of preliminary design studies and one-half upon delivery of

the finished artwork.

4. Any and all artwork created pursuant to this agreement shall be considered a

Work For Hire and the Client shall be the sole owner of the original artwork and all rights, including copyright.

5. Artist warrants that he is the creator of the Work specified here, the Work has not been published previously, that it does not infringe on any right of copyright or personal rights and rights of privacy of any person or entity and that any necessary permissions have been obtained.

6. Artist agrees he is working as an independent free-lance contractor and will be responsible for payment of all expense incurred in preparation of the Work.

Construction of the agreement shall be governed by the State of _____.

Client_____

Artist_____

Date_____

Sample Licensing Contract

A word of caution: this sample licensing agreement is NOT presented as the perfect example of the instrument, nor as an industry standard. If a potential client offers a contract that is composed in such a manner that the artist is unable to completely understand everything contained in it, consult an attorney.

Most of the companies that license imagery for use on their own products will have their own standard licensing contract. It is up to the artist to read every word of that contract and make sure he understands exactly what rights he is signing away and what rights he is retaining. When in doubt, consult an attorney.

And remember, a bad license is probably worse than no license.

Sample Licensing Agreement for Licensing Images to Users

1.0 Parties
'The Licenser' (Name and address of the Artist)
'The Licensee' (Name and address of Client)
1.1 Definitions
1.1.1 'Artwork' means transparency, positive, negative, electronic scan, work of art, painting, montage, drawing, engraving, work of artistic craftsmanship, rough drawing or rough creations or any other representations of the Licensers property or any part thereof including any representation consisting of a recording or light or other radiation or electronic signal on any medium on which an image is produced or from which an image may by any means be produced including any film or storage in a computer and

artistic merit shall not be any consideration in determining what constitutes artwork.

1.1.2 'Net Receipts' all income accruing to the Licensee from the exploitation of the Rights as hereinafter defined excluding any vat payable thereon and after the deduction of all costs and charges and expenses properly and reasonably incurred in connection with their exploitation as set out in Schedule II of this Agreement or otherwise agreed in writing between the Licenser and the Licensee on a product by product basis.

1.1.3 'Licensers Property' the property of the licenser as notified in writing by the Licenser to the Licensee.

1.1.4 ''Merchandised products' those products, designs and publications which use under the license all or part of the Artwork or images derived therefrom and referred to as the Subject Matter of this Agreement

1.1.5 'the Rights' the exclusive right by way of license for the Licenser to produce reproduce, publish sell and distribute and further to grant the non-exclusive right to the Licensee to manufacture package distribute market and sell or publish the Merchandised Product in the Territory

1.1.6 'the Territory' means the geographic areas as specified in Schedule II

2.0 Recitals: whereas (i) the Licenser is the exclusive agent for licensing the images and Artwork of the subject Matter specified in this agreement and has the right to enter into contracts with manufacturers and suppliers to manufacture or publish merchandising products under license incorporating imagery or artwork taken from and of the Subject Matter of this Agreement (ii) The Licensee is a manufacturer distributor designer or publisher of merchandised products incorporating the images or artwork of characters, picture, images and works of the original design.

2.1 Subject Matter: The Artwork as listed and particularized in Schedule I And herein referred to in this Agreement as the Subject Matter a reproduction of which is to be incorporated in Merchandised Products manufactured distributed or published by the Licensee.

2.2 Licensee: Under this agreement the Licensee shall have the non-exclusive, non-transferable, revocable right to manufacture distribute design or publish Merchandised Products based on and incorporating images of the Artwork being the Subject Matter of this agreement. This Agreement shall remain in force until Either all the Merchandised Products made or derived from the Subject Matter are sold whereupon a statement confirming all sales and receipts shall be supplied to the Licenser OR where the Licenser gives 6 months written notice of termination OR upon the expiry of the contracted period of the Agreement as specified on the invoice or in Schedule II

2.3 Consideration: The Licensee agrees to pay to the Licenser a fee as specified on the invoice and / or in Schedule II

2.4 Licensers Obligations: The Licenser warrants that it owns the license to the Rights to this Agreement and that it has the right to enter into this Agreement and that there is no present claim or litigation in respect of those Rights relating to the Subject Matter.

2.5 Licensee's Obligations:

(i) The Licensee agrees that the Licenser shall in its absolute discretion be entitled to approve all material of the Artwork and Merchandised Product prior to production, manufacture and distribution and the Licensee acknowledges that such approval must be in writing.

(ii) The Licensee confirms that a comprehensive public and product liability insurance policy is and will be in force covering any claims actions or damages which may arise as a direct or indirect result of the use by the public of the Merchandised Products.

(iii) The Licensee undertakes that the Merchandised Products will not be offensive or
obscene in nature or derogatory of any third party and will not expose the Licenser to civil or criminal proceedings.

(iv) The Licensee will use its best endeavors to ensure that the Merchandised Products do not contain any material which
infringes the copyright or design rights of any third party.

(v) The Licensee acknowledges and agrees to ensure that all third parties to be contracted by the Licensee in respect of the Merchandised Products incorporating images of the Artwork will agree that all copyright and any other rights concerning the same together with any goodwill are and shall remain the sole property of the Licenser.

(vi) The Licensee shall not sell or consign for sale any Merchandised Product outside the Territory unless with the prior written consent of the Licenser.

(vii) The Licensee shall provide the Licenser with an annual audited statement recording complete accounting details of such of its income and expenditure as is relevant for the purpose for calculating the Licenser's receipts from this Agreement in such instances where payment is calculated on a royalty basis.

(viii) The Licensee hereby unconditionally and irrevocably undertakes to indemnify the Licenser against all actions proceedings claims damages reasonable costs and
losses whatsoever made against or incurred by the Licenser in consequence of any breach by the Licensee of any term of this agreement.

2.6 Quality and Design of Merchandised Product: The Licensee undertakes and agrees that the Merchandised

Product shall be of a high standard and of such style appearance and quality as to be suited to exploitation to the best advantage of the Artwork and to protect and enhance the value of the Licenser's Property and the goodwill relating to it.

2.7 Promotional Material: The cost of promotional material and Artwork to be used by the Licensee in connection with the Merchandised Product shall be borne solely by the Licensee. The Licenser shall have the right but not the obligation to use the name of the Licensee in any publicity or advertising relating to the Merchandised Product.

2.8 Infringement: In the event of infringement of either the copyright or the Licenser's rights by any third party the Licensee will take all reasonable steps in assisting the Licenser to take such action as may in the Licenser's sole discretion be required to protect those rights.

2.9 Credits: The Licensee will ensure that the words " By Courtesy of The Art Business " or such other words and if appropriate the Licenser's logo as the Licenser shall direct shall be included on all Merchandised Products

2.10 Entire Agreement: This Agreement in conjunction with the Terms & Conditions of Submission and Reproduction of Images constitutes the entire understanding between the parties and supersedes any arrangements, understandings, promises or agreements made or existing between the parties prior to or simultaneously with these Agreements. No variation of this Agreement shall be effective unless it is in writing and signed by and on behalf of both parties.

2.11 Governing Law: This Agreement shall be governed by and construed in all respects in accordance with English Law.

3.0 Authorized signatures:

On behalf of the Licenser
Signed:
Title:
Date:

On behalf of the Licensee
Signed:
Title:
Date:

4.0 Schedule I
A detailed description of the Artwork and the Image including any attributable name and the catalogue number and recording any form or reference or coding together with details of the ownership of copyright.
4.1 Schedule II
Calculation of fees payable including
     (i) Basic price and conditions
     (ii) Quantity Discount
     (iii) Authorized Use
     (iv) Territory
     (v) Period of Use
     (vi) Terms of non-Exclusivity.
4.2 Schedule III
Any restrictions specifically required by the owner of the original image or copyright.

SAMPLE SYNDICATION CONTRACT

AGREEMENT

Name:

Date:

Dear:

The following comprises the agreement between ----- syndicate ("Syndicate") and you ("Producer") regarding our syndication of your Feature:

1) PREPARATION OF THE FEATURE.
The Producer shall prepare and furnish to the Syndicate each week during the term of this agreement, at such time prior to the Syndicate's date of release as is specified in Section 12 or otherwise as the Syndicate may reasonably specify from time to time, the following material (which, with its drawings, ideas, subject matter, format, continuity, plots, themes, characters and characterizations, is sometimes referred to as the "Feature"):

The Producer shall maintain for the Feature a quality of work consistent with that previously submitted and with the Syndicate's reasonable requirements. The title of the Feature may be changed by mutual agreement of the Producer and the Syndicate.

The original of any drawing delivered by the Producer to the Syndicate shall be the property of the Producer, and, after any such drawing has served the Syndicate's purposes, it shall be returned to the Producer. No drawing so returned

shall be published or otherwise used in any way or form which conflicts with the Syndicate's rights under
this agreement, and the return of any such drawing shall not in any way affect such rights.

2) SYNDICATION.
The Syndicate shall, in a manner consistent with customary practice in the conduct of its business, use its best efforts to sell the Feature to newspapers (both print and electronic) and shall take such other action, if any, to exploit the Feature as the Syndicate in its sole discretion deems appropriate. The Syndicate shall have absolute discretion in selecting purchasers of any rights in the Feature and in determining prices and all other terms of sale in any media. All or any part of the Syndicate's rights under this agreement may be delegated or redelegated from time to time to any sales, syndication, publication or other agency or firm, each of which may act with respect to the delegated right in its or their own name or names.

3) RIGHTS GRANTED SYNDICATE.
(a) The Syndicate shall have, and the Producer hereby transfers and conveys to the Syndicate, all copyright, proprietary and exploitation rights whatsoever in the Feature produced for the Syndicate by the Producer during the term of this agreement, including but not limited to the following exclusive rights: to reproduce the Feature in copies; to prepare derivative works based on the Feature; to distribute copies of the Feature to the public by sale or other transfer of ownership, or by rental, lease, or lending; to perform the Feature publicly; to display the Feature publicly; to trademark any name or title used in connection with any services rendered or Feature prepared or furnished under this agreement; to copyright any such Feature and to secure

any renewal of copyright permitted by law; to communicate the Feature by radio broadcasting, rebroadcasting, wired radio, television, cable, telephone, satellite or by any other methods or means (now or hereafter existing) of transmitting or delivering ideas, sounds, words, images or pictures; and to vend and otherwise dispose of, and to otherwise exercise with reference to said Feature any and all rights and privileges now and [sic] in existence or which may hereafter accrue. As used in this Section 3(a), the term "Feature" includes any derivative work based on the Feature. The Syndicate may, at its option, appoint an agent or agents to exploit one or more of the rights so granted. Whenever requested by the Syndicate, the Producer shall execute any instruments which in the judgment of the Syndicate may be necessary or desirable to secure to the Syndicate the rights granted by the agreement.

(b) The Syndicate, and its subscribers, agents and appointees, licensees and successors shall have the right to use the Producer's name, picture (color and black-and-white, provided by the Producer) and biography for promotion, trade and advertising purposes in connection with the rights granted the Syndicate hereunder.

4) EDITING: FAILURE TO DELIVER.
The Syndicate shall have the general editorial supervision of the Feature, but the Syndicate shall make no substantive changes to the Feature without the Producer's prior approval. If the Syndicate determines that a particular installment of the Feature is not suitable for publication, it shall return it to the Producer for revision and resubmission. Upon the inability (whether due to disability, death or otherwise) or the failure of the Producer to submit the Feature, suitable for publication, as determined by the

Syndicate, within such time in advance of the date of publication as the Syndicate specifies pursuant or Section 1 or Section 12, the Syndicate shall have the right, in addition to any other rights and remedies hereunder (a) in the case of late submission, to deduct from the amounts payable to Producer under this agreement all costs and expenses occasioned by such late submission (including without limitation freight, mailing and handling and overtime of personnel), and (b) in the case of non-submission, to have the Feature prepared by others, deducting the expenses incurred by it in this connection, including the compensation of a substitute writer or artist, from any amounts payable to the Producer under this agreement.

5) PRODUCER'S WARRANTIES AND INDEMNIFICATION. The Producer represents, warrants, and agrees, to and with the Syndicate and its assignees and agents, that (except to the extent attributable to editing by the Syndicate which was not approved by the Producer) all material furnished pursuant to this agreement will be original with him and that the use of such material as contemplated by this agreement will not constitute libel or conflict with or infringe upon any copyright, right of privacy or other rights of any third person or firm. The Producer will indemnify the Syndicate (and any sales, syndication, publication or other agency or firm to which the Syndicate has delegated rights under this agreement) against any expenses or damages (including reasonable attorneys' fees) resulting from any breach or alleged breach of such representation and warranty. The Syndicate and any such indemnified party shall have the right, at their discretion, either to defend any claim or suit by counsel of their choice or to settle the same on such terms as they deem advisable. In the event that a final judgment dismissing any such claim or suit without liability to the

Syndicate or any such indemnified party, the obligation of the Producer shall be limited to reimbursing the Syndicate and such indemnified party for one-half of all expenses incurred by them in connection therewith.

6) EXCLUSIVITY; RIGHTS OF FIRST REFUSAL.

During the term of this agreement, the Producer will not, without the prior written consent of the Syndicate, produce or consent to be produced (under his name or any other name or names), or advise or assist in any way with the production of, any material of similar name or appearance to the Feature for publication in any newspaper, periodical, book, or other publication. The Syndicate shall have the option to meet any bona fide offer for the services of the Producer with respect to material suitable for syndication during the term of this agreement, provided, however, that such option shall be exercised by the Syndicate within 90 days after receipt of written notice of such a bona fide offer.

7) PAYMENT TO PRODUCER.

(a) In consideration of the satisfactory performance by the Producer of his obligation under this agreement, the Syndicate shall pay to the Producer, not later than the twentieth day of each month:

(i) with respect to the sale for newspaper publication within the continental United States of the rights to the use of the Feature, 50% of the net domestic newspaper collections during the preceding month (derived by deducting from the gross collections from such sales the Syndicate's cost for in-paper promotion, sales and promotional kits, sales and commissions [not in excess of 2%], production, transportation by wire or other mechanical or electronic means, securing and protecting trademark and copyright in connection therewith);

(ii) with respect to the sale for newspaper publication outside the continental United States of the rights to the use of the Feature, 50% of the net foreign newspaper collections during the preceding month (derived by deducting from the gross collections from such sale the Syndicate's costs for agent's fees and commissions, in-paper promotion, production, trademark, copyright, and all other expenses and payments in connection therewith);

(iii) with respect to the sale of pamphlet compilations of the Feature by advertisements in the syndicated newspaper version of the Feature, 15% of the retail list price of each such pamphlet sold; and

(iv) with respect to the sale of any other rights to use, in any media or form other than newspaper publication or pamphlet sale of the Feature, or of its drawings, continuity, ideas, format, plots themes characters or characterizations, 50% of the net collections (derived by deducting from the gross collections from such sales all of the Syndicate's expenses [including without limitation agency fees and commissions] in connection therewith).

(b) The Syndicate shall render to the Producer monthly itemized statements (with remittances) of the income and disbursements of the preceding calendar month with regard to the Feature; and the Syndicate's records relating to the Feature shall be available to the Producer or his authorized Certified Public Accountants for inspection at all reasonable times during business hours.

8) PERSONAL APPEARANCES.

The Syndicate will act as the Producer's non-exclusive representative in connection with requests for personal appearances or personal services by the Producer, such as lectures, speaking engagements, television or other media appearances or advertising, product endorsements and the like, and the Syndicate will not arrange any such appearances or services for the Producer without first securing his approval, which he will not withhold unreasonably. The Producer will notify the Syndicate promptly of his approval or disapproval of the terms of appearances or services submitted to him. The Producer will pay to the Syndicate 20% of all amounts, after deducting therefrom his direct and necessary expenses incurred, which he receives for any such personal appearances or services, such payments to be made promptly after receipt of such amounts by the Producer.

9) TERM AND TERMINATION.

(a) The term of this agreement shall commence on the date hereof and end on the date ten calendar years from the date of first publication of the Feature in a newspaper, except that such term shall be automatically renewed for an additional period of ten years if the Syndicate's gross weekly billings during the first six months of the last year of the original ten-year term for the sale of the Feature and other rights granted pursuant to this agreement average at least $_____ .

(b) Beginning with the thirteenth month after the date of the first publication of the Feature in a newspaper, if the aggregate payment to the Producer (prior to any deductions pursuant to Sections 4 and 7) under this agreement during any calendar month averages less than $_____ per week, either the Producer or the Syndicate may cancel this agreement upon at least 30 days notice to the other given within the month following the month of such occurrence. Should the Producer elect to so terminate, the Syndicate may continue this agreement by advancing to the Producer a sum equal to the difference between $_____ and the aggregate payments due to the Producer (after any deductions pursuant to Sections 4 and

7) for the month upon which such election is based, and repayment of any such advance shall be made solely from subsequent payments due the Producer hereunder. No such advance shall constitute a waiver of either the Producer's or the Syndicate's right to cancel upon subsequent recurrences of the contingency provided for herein.

(c) Upon any termination of this agreement, whether by expiration or otherwise:

(i) If there are at the time of such termination any outstanding contracts to third parties respecting any rights hereunder, the Syndicate shall continue to receive the proceeds therefrom, and shall make payments to the Producer in accordance with Section 7, until such contracts are terminated. Section 9(b) shall not be applicable.

(ii) The Syndicate shall have the exclusive right to republish or cause republication in any media of all material delivered to it during the term of this agreement provided that payment is made to Producer with respect to any republication in accordance with Section 7. Section 9(b) shall not be applicable.

10) ASSIGNMENT, ETC.
This agreement shall be binding upon and inure to the benefits of the parties hereto and their respective heirs, legal representatives, successors and assigns, except that this agreement may not be assigned by the Producer except (a) to

a corporation formed by the Producer of which all of the voting stock is owned and continues to be owned by him, and (b) where the Producer continues to be the person who prepares the Feature.

11) BOOK PUBLISHING AND LICENSING.
The Syndicate is affiliated with a book publishing firm and with a licensing firm and the Syndicate may (but need not), pursuant to rights granted it by this agreement, contract with either for publication or other uses respecting the Feature. In this connection, the Syndicate will not so contract with either affiliate except on terms which (a) considering all circumstances, in the Syndicated reasonable judgment are as favorable as could be obtained from an unaffiliated party, and (b) provide creative control to the Producer and the Syndicate. Receipts by the Syndicate from either affiliate pursuant to any such contract will be subject to the payment provisions of this agreement.

12) TIME OF DELIVERY.
The time of delivery of installments of the Feature shall be set forth below or, if no time is specified, such delivery shall be as is reasonably specified by the Syndicate from time to time:
Time is of the essence as to this Section, and Section 4 contains certain provisions for deductions for costs occasioned by Producer's failure to meet delivery times. 13)

13) PRODUCT AGREEMENT.
Producer acknowledges that this agreement is not a personal services or employment agreement and that the Producer is an independent contractor and not an employee of the Syndicate.

14) GOVERNING LAW. This agreement shall be governed by the laws of the State of _____ as to all matters including, without limitation, matters of validity, construction, effect and performance.

15) MISCELLANEOUS.
If there is more than one Producer, the term "Producer" herein shall mean all of them, their obligations under this agreement shall be joint and several, and any payment due them hereunder shall be equally divided among them unless they otherwise specify by notice in writing to the Syndicate. The section headings herein are for reference only and shall not be considered in interpreting this agreement. The provisions of this agreement constitute the entire understanding of the parties hereto, and this agreement may not be amended, modified or discharged except in writing. The waiver of any party hereto to a breach of any provision of this agreement shall not operate or be construed as a waiver of any subsequent breach by any party.

To indicate your acceptance of and agreement to the foregoing, please sign and return to
us the enclosed copies of this agreement.

Very truly yours,

-----SYNDICATE

By _____
The foregoing is accepted and agreed to as of the date hereof.

(Producer)

RECOMMENDED READING

Artists & Graphic Designer's Market
Writer's Digest Books.
    This annual publication is the standard reference guide for selling, publishing and licensing art and graphic design work. It includes contact information, submission guidelines, and payment information for approximately 2,000 current markets.

Cartooning: The Art & the Business by Mort Gerberg, William Morrow & Company, 1989.
An essential guide to the cartoon art form loaded with examples from a wide variety of cartoon professionals.

The Complete Book of Humorous Art by Bob Staake, North Light Books, 1996.
Twenty top Humorous Illustration professionals talk about their professional--everything from technique to marketing.

Drawing Words & Writing Pictures
by Jessica Abel & Matt Madden
First-Second Publishing, 2008
A definitive course from concept to comic in 15 lessons

How to Draw and Sell Cartoons by Dave Breger
G.P.Putnam & Sons, 1966

An often overlooked classic treatise on the art of cartooning covering most every aspect of the form. Quite frankly, if I were only allowed one book on cartooning, this is the one. Long out of print, but often available via online resellers.

How to Draw Tips from the Top Cartoonists,
edited by Don Cristensen,
Donnar Publications, 1982.
An extraordinary reference now out of print, but easily found online. Thirty-two imminently successful cartoonists each take a couple of pages and demonstrate drawing tips and tricks-of-the-trade. Participants include Sergio Aragones, Bill Melendez, Jim Aparo, Doug Wildey, Dale Messick, Bob Oksner, Trina Robbins, Mort Walker, Mort Drucker and Gus Arriola.

Humorous Illustration by Nick Meglin,
Watson-Guptill Publications, 1989.
A serious look at the business of Humorous Illustration via conversations with cartoonists like Jack Davis, Sergio Aragones, Gerry Gersten, Arnold Roth and Maurice Sendak.

The Naked Cartoonist by Robert Mankoff
Black Dog & Levanthal Publishers, 2002.
Mankoff is the former Cartoon Editor of the New Yorker. This book draws on his vast experience exploring methods of enhancing creativity, honing your wit, getting great
ideas and being more creative every day.

Understanding Comics and ***Making Comics***
by Scott McCloud
Harper Publishing, 1993 & 2006 (respectively)
Standard tomes on the art of comic book and graphic novel creation.

The Webcomics Handbook *by Brad Guigar*
Toonhound Studios, 2014
Massive tutorial based on Brad Guigar's four years of writing at Webcomics.com covers the art, business, and promotion of digital comics. With chapters devoted to website basics, digital downloads, social media, advertising, business, and much more.

Your Career in the Comics by Lee Nordling
Andrews & McMeel Publishers, 1995.
Detailed information on the business of being a professional cartoonist, with emphasis on
newspaper comic strip and panel syndication.

WEB RESOURCES

Art Business News
http://www.artbusinessncws.com/
Art Business News is a trade publication for the gallery and interior-design retail markets.

Cafe Press
http://www.cafepress.com/
 Online POD marketplace where you can create sell made-to-order custom products from your artwork, such as posters and prints and various items of apparel.

Comic Book Resources
http://www.comicbookresources.com/
Comic Book Resources (CBR) is the leading comic book web site. Renowned for its high quality content and active community, CBR draws the most loyal audience of users. The site links to some 1700 comic book sites, including publishers, creators and fan sites.

Comic Publisher Submission Guidelines
https://jasonthibault.com/definitive-list-comic-publisher-submission-guidelines/
Definitive list of comic book publishers, book and magazine publishers and newspaper syndicates with links to submission guidelines.

CreateSpace div of Amazon
https://www.createspace.com/
Print on Demand site for self-publishing comics and graphic novels. There is no startup cost involved in creating your book and Amazon will list it for sale on their worldwide sites.

Diamond Distributors
http://www.diamondcomics.com/
The primary comic book distributor website. Includes the current catalog, as well as guidelines for submitting a book for distribution consideration.

Go Comics
http://www.gocomics.com/
Online syndicated newspaper comics.

Literary Agents Representing Graphic Novels
http://niki-smith.com/about/graphic-novel-agents/
A list of Literary Agents who represent Graphic Novels and Comics.

LuLu
http://www.lulu.com/
themes/create/homepage.php
On demand book, calendar and image printer.

Luna Pic
http://www141.lunapic.com/editor/
Free web-based basic graphics editor.

National Cartoonists Society
http://www.reuben.org

Home and birthplace of the famed Reuben Awards, this organization is the premiere professional cartoonist association.

Pixlr
https://pixlr.com/editor/
Free web-based graphics editor operationally similar to Photoshop.

Red Bubble
https://www.redbubble.com/
Online marketplace where you can create sell made-to-order custom products from your artwork, such as posters and prints and various items of apparel.

Zazzle
http://www.zazzle.com/
Online marketplace where you can create sell made-to-order custom products from your artwork, such as posters and prints and various items of apparel.

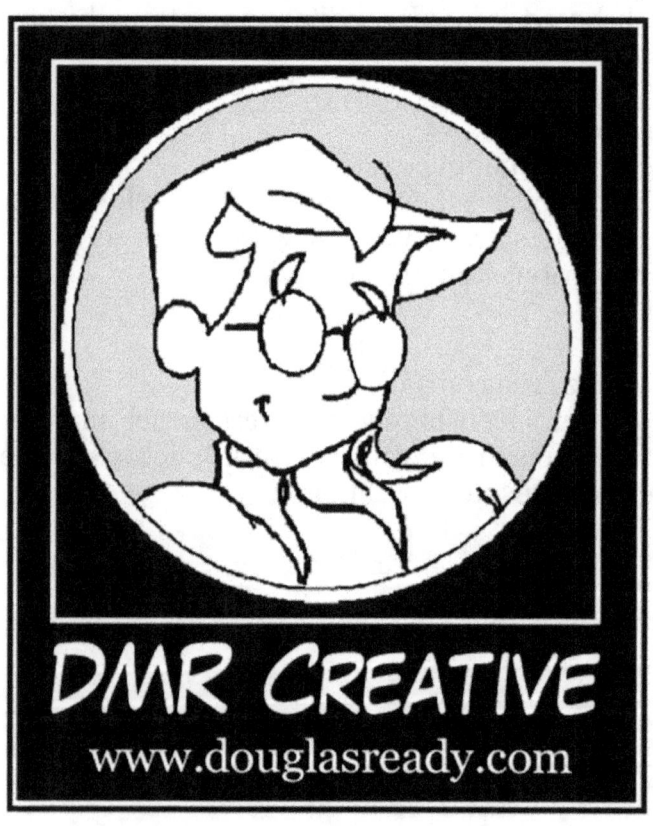

Douglas Ready has worked professionally for more than thirty years as a cartoonist, illustrator, product designer and author.

Doug has produced illustrations for advertising, books, magazines, greeting cards, posters and coloring books and is the creator of the comic features *Beach Drive* and *AKA Morgue.* He's taught cartooning in a number of venues, including a course at the University of South Carolina.

Doug also does product design work, creating plush toys, puppets and puzzles, and a variety of consumer paper products such as party and holiday paper plates and cups, napkins, novelties and party favors.

Doug is the author of a series of thriller novels chronicling the adventures of Private Investigator Micah Frost. *Frost* and *Second Shot* are currently available via **Amazon**, and the third, *A Very Blue Moon* is scheduled for release in December, 2017.

Doug is the also author of two other art business books, *The Greeting Card Business Manual* and *Selling Your Art*, and a volume of humorous verse titled *The Laid-Off Blues and Other Cautionary Rhymes* (all available on **Amazon**).

Doug's self-directed work is published and marketed via *DMR Creative*. He is a former partner in *Carousel Studios* and the former owner of *Studio 5*, both commercial art firms specialized in product design, greeting card and poster creation, licensing and publishing.

Doug and his incredible wife Mona live in the Pacific Northwest.

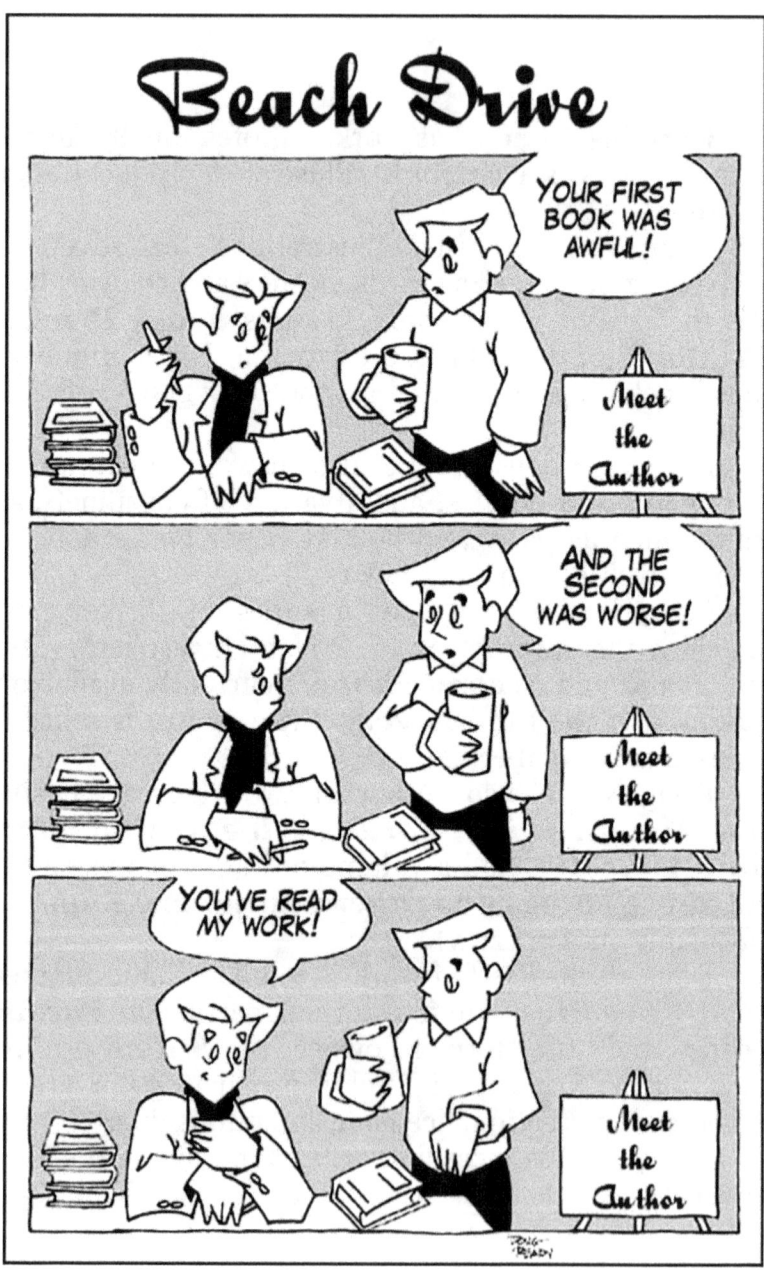

www.ingramcontent.com/pod-product-compliance
Lightning Source LLC
Chambersburg PA
CBHW051547170526
45165CB00002B/917